NAOMI IN THE LIVING ROOM and Other Short Plays

A COLLECTION OF ONE-ACTS BY
CHRISTOPHER DURANG

★

★

DRAMATISTS
PLAY SERVICE
INC.

NAOMI IN THE LIVING ROOM & OTHER SHORT PLAYS
Copyright © 1998, Christopher Durang

NAOMI IN THE LIVING ROOM
Copyright © 1991, Christopher Durang

All Rights Reserved

Photo by Susan Johann

Sherry Anderson, John Augustine and Deborah LaCoy in a scene from the Home for Contemporary Theatre production of *Naomi in the Living Room*.

NAOMI IN THE LIVING ROOM
& OTHER SHORT PLAYS

I've been intending to publish this volume of miscellaneous short plays for a long time.

This volume has nine plays that are not presently available anywhere else. The nine new ones are: KITTY THE WAITRESS, GYM TEACHER, NOT MY FAULT, AUNT DAN MEETS THE MAD-WOMAN OF CHAILLOT, CARDINAL O'CONNOR, ENTER-TAINING MR. HELMS, THE DOCTOR WILL SEE YOU NOW, UNDER DURESS, and AN ALTAR BOY TALKS TO GOD.

I have separated the plays in this volume into three cate-gories — character comedies, parodies, and political plays.

The first 13 plays, starting with NAOMI IN THE LIVING ROOM and ending with NOT MY FAULT, I am calling "charac-ter" comedies and sketches ... the humor in them is usually to be found in the strange sensibilities that these characters have, and how the more "normal" characters react to them.

The next four plays are parodies — of the Hardy Boys, of MEDEA, of Wallace Shawn's play AUNT DAN AND LEMON, and of Tennessee Williams. (In the DPS volume DURANG/DURANG, I also have parodies of Williams and of Sam Shepard.)

And the final six plays are political plays — sketches or scenes that I was inspired to write due to some political issue or other.

As some of you know, I like to write author's notes, especially about acting tone, and about clarifying issues that actors and di-rectors may come upon when doing my work.

For this volume, I am choosing to write fewer of these notes ... the pieces are often so short, I feel foolish writing notes that are longer than the pieces. So when I've written notes, it's when I feel a piece is particularly open to misinterpretation.

An additional thought — for those of you looking to do a full evening of my short plays, I thought I'd tell you what kinds of play combinations have been done so far.

In 1994 Manhattan Theatre Club did six one-acts of mine under the title DURANG/DURANG (and published by DPS under that title). Act One was MRS. SORKEN (a monologue), FOR WHOM THE SOUTHERN BELLE TOLLS (a parody of Williams' THE GLASS MENAGERIE), A STYE OF THE EYE (a parody of Sam Shepard's A LIE OF THE MIND). Act Two was NINA IN THE MORNING, WANDA'S VISIT, and BUSINESS LUNCH AT THE RUSSIAN TEA ROOM.

In 1996 the director David Chambers put together a different grouping of pieces at South Coast Repertory that we decided to call A MESS OF PLAYS BY CHRIS DURANG. Act One was JOHN AND MARY DOE, WOMAN STAND-UP, NINA IN THE MORNING, THE GYM TEACHER, CARDINAL O'CONNOR and NAOMI IN THE LIVING ROOM (for a rousing close to the act). Act Two was FUNERAL PARLOR, AN ALTAR BOY TALKS TO GOD, and FOR WHOM THE SOUTHERN BELLE TOLLS. A snappy closing musical number, using particularly notable costumed characters from the evening, was concocted.

And in June 1997, Tracey Becker and Nellie Bellflower produced four weekends of theatre called CHAMPAGNE AND SUNSET at the John Drew Theatre in East Hampton, New York. For the final weekend, they presented an evening of one acts by me, called MIX AND MATCH DURANG, directed by Elizabeth Gottlieb. Act One was DESIRE, DESIRE, DESIRE, THE HARDY BOYS AND THE MYSTERY OF WHERE BABIES COME FROM, and NAOMI IN THE LIVING ROOM. Act Two was KITTY THE WAITRESS, FUNERAL PARLOR, GYM TEACHER and BUSINESS LUNCH AT THE RUSSIAN TEA ROOM.

Anyway, as you can see, it is possible to indeed mix and match among these plays (and the six in the DURANG/DU-RANG volume), and to create an evening that best suits your actors' talents and interests.

The trick in choosing is how to mix the moods right; many of my plays are frenetic and loud, and it's probably a good idea to mix in plays that have softer, quieter tones too.

Along those lines, in the East Hampton evening, the two plays that most pleased the audience seemed to be FUNERAL PARLOR and BUSINESS LUNCH AT THE RUSSIAN TEA

4

ROOM — I think because both had main characters who were sympathetic and that the audience could care about. NAOMI IN THE LIVING ROOM also went especially well (as it did at South Coast Repertory). NAOMI, though, is like riding a roller coaster; and I think for the balance of the evening it's important to include the softer emotions to be found in FUNERAL PARLOR and BUSINESS LUNCH.

Well, anyway, here's this volume of lots of short plays. I hope you enjoy them.

Christopher Durang
July 15, 1998

TABLE OF CONTENTS

NAOMI IN THE LIVING ROOM

NAOMI IN THE LIVING ROOM was first presented by HOME FOR CONTEMPORARY THEATRE (Randy Rollison, Denise Lancot; Artistic Directors) in New York City, in December, 1988, on a bill of plays set in the living room by Eve Ensler, John PiRoman and Barry Kaplan. It was directed by the author. The productions all shared the same set, designed by Geoff MacStutis. The cast was as follows:

NAOMI ....Sherry Anderson
JOHN...John Augustine
JOHNNA ....Elizabeth Alley

It was subsequently performed again at HOME in 1989 where Deborah LaCoy played the part of JOHNNA for two performances. It was at Ensemble Studio Theatre, in New York City, as part of their one-act marathon 1990. The cast was the same, though Ms. Alley was unable to play her part at E.S.T., and so Ilene Kristen played JOHNNA in that production.

Other notable productions include at South Coast Repertory in Costa Mesa, California (as part of A MESS OF PLAYS BY CHRIS DURANG in 1996), with Jodi Thelen as NAOMI, Robert Patrick Benedict as JOHN, and Amanda Carlin as JOHNNA, directed by David Chambers. And in 1997 at the John Drew Theatre in East Hampton, New York (as part of MIX AND MATCH DURANG presented by Birnam Wood), with Jennifer Van Dyck as NAOMI, Michael Ian Black as JOHN, Penny Balfour as JOHNNA, directed by Elizabeth Gottlieb.

CHARACTERS

NAOMI
JOHN
JOHNNA, his wife

NAOMI IN THE
LIVING ROOM

Scene: A living room. Enter Naomi, followed by John and Johnna, an attractive young couple. John has a moustache and is dressed in a suit and tie. Johnna is wearing a dress with a string of pearls. Naomi, though, looks odd.

Naomi plants herself somewhere definitive — by the mantelpiece, for instance — and gestures out toward the room.

NAOMI.   And this is the living room. And you've seen the dining room, and the bedroom, and the bathroom.
JOHN.   Yes, I know. I used to live here.
NAOMI.   The dining room is where we dine. The bedroom is where we go to bed. The bathroom is where we take a bath. The kitchen is where we ... cook. That doesn't sound right. The kitchen is where we ... collect kitsch. Hummel figurines, Statue of Liberty salt and pepper shakers, underpants that say Home of the Whopper, and so on. Kitsch. The kitchen is where we look at kitsch. The laundry room is where we do laundry. And the living room is where Hubert and I do all of our living. Our major living. So that's the living room.
JOHNNA.   What do you use the cellar for?
NAOMI.   *(Suspicious.)* What?
JOHNNA.   What do you use the cellar for?
NAOMI.   We use the cellar to ... we go to the cellar to ... replenish our cells. We go to the attic to ... practice our tics, our facial tics. *(Her face contorts variously.)* And we go to the car port, to port the car. Whew! Please don't ask me any more questions, I'm afraid I may not have the strength to find the answers. *(Laughs uproariously.)* Please, sit down, don't let my manner make you uncomfortable. Sit on one of the sitting devices, we use them for sitting in the living room. *(There is a couch and one*

chair to choose from. John and Johnna go to sit on the couch. Naomi screams at them:) DON'T SIT THERE, I WANT TO SIT THERE!!! *(John and Johnna stand and look frightened. Naomi charges over to the couch, and John and Johnna almost have to run to avoid being sat on by her.)* Shits! Ingrates! It's my house, it's my living room. I didn't ask you, I can ask you to leave. *(John and Johnna are still standing, and start to maybe edge out of the room.)* No, no, sit down. Please, make yourselves at home, this is the living room, it's where Rupert and I do all our living. *(There's only one chair, so with some hesitation Johnna sits in the chair, and John stands behind her. Naomi stretches her arms out on the couch.)* Wow. Boy oh boy. I need a big couch to sit on because I'M A BIG PERSONALITY!!!! *(Laughs uproariously.)* Tell me, are you two ever going to speak, or do I just have to go on and on by myself, or WHAT!!!!!! *(Naomi stares at John and Johnna intensely. They hesitate but then speak.)*

JOHNNA.   This is a very comfortable chair. I love it.

JOHN.   Yes, thank you.

NAOMI.   Go on.

JOHNNA.   Ummmm, this morning I washed my hair, and then I dried it. And we had coffee in the kitchen, didn't we, John?

JOHN.   Yes, Johnna, we did.

JOHNNA.   *(Pause, doesn't know what else to say.)* And I love sitting in this chair.

NAOMI.   I think I want to sit in it, get up, get up. *(Naomi charges over, and John and Johnna move away from it, standing uncomfortably. Naomi sits and moves around in the chair, luxuriating in it.)* Hmmmm, yes. Chair, chair. Chair in the living room. Hmmm, yes. *(Looks at John and Johnna, shouts at them:)* Well, go sit down on the fucking couch, you morons! *(John and Johnna look startled, and sit on the couch. Naomi screams offstage.)* Leonard! Oh, Leonard! Come on in here in the living room and have some conversation with us. You don't want me to soak up everything our son says all by myself, do you? *(Naomi stands and walks over to John and Johnna on the couch. She smiles at Johnna.)* You probably didn't know John was Herbert's and my son, did you?

JOHNNA.   Yes, he told me. I've met you before, you know.

NAOMI.   Shut up! *(Calls out.)* Hubert! Rupert! Leonard! *(To John and Johnna.)* I hope he's not dead. I wouldn't know

14

what room to put him in. We don't have a dead room. *(Smiles; screams.)* AAAAAAAAAAAAAAAAAAAHHHHHHHHH! *(Looks at them.)* Goodness, my moods switch quickly. *(Naomi sees a tiny stuffed pig in a Santa Claus suit perched on the mantelpiece. With momentary interest, she picks it up and looks at it, then puts it down again. Focusing on John and Johnna again; a good hostess.)* Tell me all about yourselves, do you have children? *(Sits, listens attentively.)*

JOHNNA. We had five children but they all died in a car accident. The baby sitter was taking them for a ride, and she was drunk. We were very upset.

NAOMI. Uh huh. Do you like sitting on the couch?

JOHN. Mother, Johnna was telling you something sad.

NAOMI. Was she? I'm sorry, Johnna, tell it to me again.

JOHNNA. We had five children ...

NAOMI. *(Tries to concentrate, but something impinges on her consciousness.)* Wait a minute, something's bothering me!!!! *(She rushes over to the little stuffed Santa pig, snatches it up and throws it against the wall in a fury.)* This belongs in the kitchen, *not* in the living room. The living room is for living, it is not meant for sincerely designed but ludicrously corny artifacts! Kitsch! *(She sits down again.)* Do you like Hummel figurines?

JOHN. Very much. Now that the children are dead, Johnna and I have begun to collect Hummel figurines, especially little boy shepherds and little girl shepherdesses.

NAOMI. Uh, huh, isn't that interesting? Excuse me if I fall asleep. I'm not tired yet, but I just want to apologize in advance in case your boring talk puts me to sleep. I don't want to offend you. *(Screams.)* AAAAAAAAAAAAAAAAAHHHHHHHHH! I'm just so bored I could scream. Did you ever hear that expression? AAAAAAAAAAAAAAAAHHHHHHHHHHH!

JOHN. Excuse me, I want to change my clothes. I'm tired of my color scheme. Do you have a clothes changing room?

NAOMI. No, I don't have a clothes changing room, you certainly are an idiot. Use the bedroom or the bathroom. Really, children these days have no sense. In my day we killed them.

JOHN. *(To Johnna.)* Excuse me, I'll be right back.

JOHNNA. Must you go?

JOHN. Darling, I don't feel comfortable in these colors. They're hurting my eyes.

JOHNNA. Well, bring it back.

JOHN. What?

JOHNNA. *(Sincere, confused.)* I'm sorry, I don't know what I mean. *(John exits.)* He's constantly talking about his color scheme. It's my cross to bear, I guess. That and the death of the children.

NAOMI. So who the fuck are you, anyway?

JOHNNA. I'm Johnna. I'm married to your son. All our children recently were killed.

NAOMI. Stop talking about your children, I heard you the first time. God, some people can't get over their own little personal tragedies, what a great big crashing boor. Lots of people have it worse, girlie, so eat shit! *(Calls offstage.)* Hey, John, where did you get this turd of a wife, at the Salvation Army? I'd bring her back! *(Laughs uproariously.)* Ahahahahahahahaha!

JOHNNA. I think I want to go.

NAOMI. Boy, you can't take criticism, can you? Sit down, let's have a conversation. This is the conversation pit. You can't leave the pit until you converse on at least five subjects with me. Starting now, go: *(Waits expectantly.)*

JOHNNA. I was reading about Dan Quayle's grandmother the other day.

NAOMI. That's one. Go on.

JOHNNA. She said there should be prayer in the schools ...

NAOMI. That's two. *(Naomi starts to remove her boots, or high heeled shoes, in order to massage her feet.)*

JOHNNA. And that we should have a strong defense ...

NAOMI. That's three.

JOHNNA. And that the Supreme Court should repeal the *Wade vs. Roe* ruling that legalized abortions.

NAOMI. That's four.

JOHNNA. And that even in the case of pregnancy resulting from incest, she felt that the woman should be forced to carry the child through to term.

NAOMI. That's four-A.

JOHNNA. And then she said she hoped the mother would be

forced to suffer and slave over a horrible job and take home a tiny teeny paycheck to pay for some hovel somewhere, and live in squalor with the teeny tiny baby, and that then she hoped she'd be sorry she ever had sexual intercourse.

NAOMI. That's still four-A.

JOHNNA. Don't you think she's lacking in Christian charity?

NAOMI. That's five, kind of. Yes, I do. But then so few people are true Christians anymore. I know I'm not. I'm a psychotic. *(She throws her boot in Johnna's direction.)* Get up off the couch, I want to sit there. *(Naomi rushes over, Johnna has to vacate fast. Then Naomi starts to luxuriate in sitting in the couch, moving sensuously. Naomi luxuriates all over it.)* Oh, couch, couch, big couch in the living room. I have room to spread. Couch, couch, you are my manifest destiny. Mmmmm, yes, yes. *(Calls out.)* Edward, hurry out here, I'm about to have an orgasm, you don't want to miss it. *(Back to herself.)* Mmmmmm, yes, couch, couch pillows, me sitting on the couch in the living room, mmmmm, yes, mmmm … no. *(Calls.)* Forget it! It's not happening. *(To Johnna.)* Tell me, can you switch moods like I can? Let me see you. *(Johnna stares for a moment.)* No, go ahead, try.

JOHNNA. Very well. *(Happy.)* I'm so happy, I'm so happy. *(Screams.)* AAAAAAAH! Do you have chocolates for me? *(Desperate.)* I'm so sad, I'm so sad. Drop dead! *(Laughs hysterically.)* Ahahahahahahahaha! That's a good one! *(Looks at Naomi for feedback.)*

NAOMI. Very phoney, I didn't believe you for a moment. *(Calls offstage.)* Herbert! Are you there? *(To Johnna.)* Tell me, do you think Shubert is dead?

JOHNNA. You mean the composer?

NAOMI. Is he a composer? *(Calls out.)* Lanford, are you a composer? *(Listens.)* He never answers. That's why I sometimes worry he might be dead and, as I said, I don't have a room for a dead person. We might build one on, and that would encourage the economy and prove the Republicans right, but I don't understand politics, do you?

JOHNNA. Politics?

NAOMI. Politics, politics! What, are you deaf? Are you stupid? Are you dead? Are you sitting in a chair? *(Enter John. He is*

17

dressed just like Johnna — the same dress, pearls, stockings, shoes. He has shaved off his moustache, and he wears a wig that resembles her hair, and has a bow in it like the one she has in her hair. They look very similar.)

JOHN. Hello again.

NAOMI. You took off your moustache.

JOHN. I just feel so much better this way.

NAOMI. Uh huh.

JOHNNA. *(Deeply embarrassed.)* John and I are in couples therapy because of this. Dr. Cucharacha says his cross-dressing is an intense kind of co-dependence.

NAOMI. If this Dr. Cucharacha cross-dresses, I wouldn't see him. That's what John here is doing. Too many men in women's clothing, nothing gets done!

JOHNNA. *(To John.)* Why do you humiliate me so this way?

JOHN. I want to be just like you. Say something so I can copy you.

JOHNNA. Oh, John. *(Does a feminine gesture and looks away.)*

JOHN. Oh, John. *(Imitates her gesture.)* That doesn't give me much. Say something else.

JOHNNA. Maybe it's in your genes.

JOHN. Maybe it's in your genes. *(Johnna, in her discomfort, keeps touching her hair, her pearls, shaking her head, etc. John imitates everything she does, glowing with glee. His imitations drive her crazy, and is undoubtedly part of what has them in couples therapy.)*

NAOMI. This is a disgusting sight. *(Calls.)* Sherbert, our son is prancing out here with his wife, you should really see this. *(To them.)* I find this uncomfortable. This make me want to vomit.

JOHNNA. Maybe we should go.

JOHN. Maybe we should go.

NAOMI. *(Upset.)* How come you don't dress like me? How come you dress like her?

JOHN. I want to be noticed, but I don't want to be considered insane.

JOHNNA. John, please, just stay quiet and pose if you must, but no more talking.

NAOMI. Insane? Is he referring to someone in this room as

insane? *(Calls.)* Sally! Gretchen! Marsha! Felicity! *(To John and Johnna.)* I'm calling my army in here, and then we'll have some dead bodies.

JOHNNA.   Maybe we should go.

JOHN.   Maybe we should go. *(Keeps imitating Johnna's movements.)*

JOHNNA.   Will you stop that? *(Naomi, very upset and discombobulated, stands on the couch and begins to pace up and down on it.)*

NAOMI.   Insane, I'll give you insane! What's the capital of Madagascar? You don't know, do you? Now who's insane? What's the square root of 347? You don't know, do you? Well, get out of here, if you think I'm so crazy. If you want to dress like her and not like me, I don't want you here. *(Naomi lies down on the couch in a snit to continue her upset. John begins to stride back and forth around the room, pretending he's on a fashion runway. Johnna slumps back in her chair and covers her eyes.)* I can have Christmas by myself, I can burn the Yule log by myself, I can wait for Santa by myself. I can pot geraniums. I can bob for apples. I can buy a gun in a store and shoot you. By myself! Do you get it? *(Stands and focuses back on them.)* You're dead meat with me, both of you. You're ready for the crock pot. You're a crock of shit. Leave here. I don't need you, and you're dead! *(Pause.)*

JOHNNA.   Well, I guess we should be going.

JOHN.   Well, I guess we should be going. *(Johnna and John, looking the same and walking the same, leave the house. Naomi chases after them to the door.)*

NAOMI.   Fuck you and the horse you came in on! *(John and Johnna exit. Naomi comes back into the room and is overcome with grief. She sits back on the couch and lets out enormous, heartfelt sobs. They go on for a quite a bit, but when they subside she's like an infant with a new thought, and she seems to be fairly contented.)* Well, that was a nice visit.

PROPERTY LIST

Stuffed pig in Santa Clause suit (NAOMI)

AUTHOR'S NOTE

Afterword

In 1988 I was asked to write a short play for the on-going "home" series at the Home for Contemporary Theatre in Soho. For each evening of this series, the artistic directors chose a room in the "home," and then asked authors to write plays taking place in that room. And so far they'd already had evenings of plays set in the bedroom, and in the kitchen, and now they were up the living room.

When I thought about what to write, my mind went to actress Sherry Anderson, whom I had just seen in a play reading where she acted Phyllis Diller in a nightmare. She didn't do an imitation; because it was a nightmare scene, she played the part as this really odd character with a pink wig and turquoise blue dress, who had a crazy glint in her eye and some sort of inner logic that you could tell she followed, even if you didn't.

I felt the character Sherry came up with had nothing really to do with Phyllis Diller, but was a creation of her own. And I felt this desire to write something for her to play this irrational character.

And since this was to be part of the "living room" series, in my mind I heard this clunky first line of "And this is the living room." And then the character going on to explain each additional room of the house.

I knew Sherry through my good friend John Augustine — they grew up in Canton, Ohio together — and so I wrote a part for John, and for our friend Elizabeth Alley as well. (John and Sherry also play "Dawne" in my crackpot cabaret act, CHRIS DURANG AND DAWNE.)

NAOMI was the final play of the evening, after plays by Eve Ensler, John PiRoman and Barry Kaplan. And the play went over great with this downtown audience; all three actors were terrific, and Sherry in particular was outstanding as this really odd woman.

21

In describing her take on the character, I think of the Monty Python actors playing women — it had that kind of exaggeration, yet she also had this believable look in her eye that truly crazy people do — everything she said and thought made perfect sense to her. And she was a force of nature. When she offered a seat, but then suddenly screamed that no, she wanted to sit there, and charged at them like a suddenly furious rhino — I found her hilarious.

The play was a "hit" at HOME; and when they had an evening of the best of the HOME series, we re-did the play again.

It was great fun doing this play at HOME. Later we did it again at Ensemble Studio Theatre, and it worked some of the time, getting good laughs, but then other times sat there like a big mess, with a mostly silent, baffled audience. It was very disorienting. Different theatre, different aura, different order (we were first, and maybe the play is too weird to be first; it's better as a nutty dessert).

So we prefer to remember the two times we did the play at HOME.

Some thoughts for actors approaching the play:

Naomi is a "large" character. She needs to be able to shout, and run around the room, and be very inconsistent. She must find an inner logic where all this makes sense … she's rather like an infant, who changes its focus with total concentration from moment to moment, but with little sense of continuity. One minute she's fine, the next minute she's angry at something and screaming, the next minute she's over it. When the people around her are still upset by her outbursts, she has no understanding of that; she has an infant's sense of time and appropriateness.

John and Johnna are important parts; they both are the normative figures, and the play needs their normal presence to set off Naomi's craziness. As John Augustine and Elizabeth Alley played the parts, John was initially doing his best not to react in irritation to his mother, but had a certain just-holding-the-lid-on impatience listening to her; and Johnna, less familiar with the mother and more drawn to people-pleasing, was more willing to make nice and overlook really odd things.

When John disappears and comes back in drag, John Augustine played these sections in sheer delight; he was pleased as punch to be in this other reality where he got to imitate his wife's way of dressing, her way of moving, etc. At that point he seemed as crazy as his mother, though not hostile.

Johnna's continuing attempt to act normal and make the best of things is very important to the last part of the play; she's the only "normal" one left at that point, and the other two characters need her discomforted reactions to bounce off of.

As for Naomi in the last third of the play, Sherry seemed to play a disassociated irritation at John's drag — she didn't exactly mind (or even quite notice) that he's now in a dress, instead she seemed grouchy and dissatisfied about something larger that was nagging at her — probably the fact that now that he's in a dress and striding all over the room, she senses that he's getting more attention than before, and this doesn't make her happy. And she strikes out at them unreasonably, her sense of well being all discombobulated.

Well, it's a silly, high energy, funny (I hope) play. Good luck. Make of it what you can.

KITTY THE WAITRESS

KITTY THE WAITRESS was first presented in an evening called NINE LIVES at the Juilliard School, Drama Division, in New York City, on February 21 and 22, 1997. The evening was a series of nine plays, all about the lives of a cat. The other eight plays were by Hilary Bell, Ron Fitzgerald, Daniel Goldfarb, Jessica Goldberg, Bob Kerr, David Lindsay-Abaire, Marsha Norman, and Alexandra Tolk. The evening was directed by Elizabeth Gottlieb; the program coordinator was Richard Feldman; and production stage manager was Scott Rollison. The cast for KITTY THE WAITRESS was:

HOSTESS ....Claire Lautier
MR. O'BRIEN...Peter Jacobson
KITTY ....Greg McFadden*
WAITER ....Erin Gann
VERONIQUE ....Pamela Nyberg
VETERINARIAN ....Dave Case

*NOTE: The part of KITTY is meant to be played by a woman. For the purpose of the NINE LIVES evening, we chose to have the cat in each play played by the same actor, necessitating having a male actor play the waitress in my play and a fading female cat star in Bob Kerr's play. The other seven plays all had a male cat in them. Greg McFadden did a terrific job as the waitress in my play; but especially if you present the play on its own, I prefer that KITTY be played by a woman.

Subsequent to this production, KITTY THE WAITRESS was included in the evening MIX AND MATCH DURANG, presented by Birnam Wood, Tracey Becker and Nellie Bellflower, producers, at the John Drew Theatre, in East Hampton, New York, on June 27 and 28, 1997. The evening was directed by Elizabeth Gottlieb. The cast was as follows:

HOSTESS .... Claire Lautier
MR. O'BRIEN .... Peter Jacobson
KITTY .... Penny Balfour
WAITER .... Michael Ian Black
VERONIQUE .... Jennifer Van Dyck
VETERINARIAN .... Jonathan Walker

CHARACTERS

THE HOSTESS, gracious and French
MR. O'BRIEN, American
KITTY, the waitress, seductive and French
THE WAITER
VERONIQUE, another waitress
THE VETERINARIAN

KITTY THE WAITRESS

Scene: A restaurant on a tropical island. An American man, Mr. O'Brien, enters. He is in his early 30s to early 40s. He is greeted by a friendly, effusive French woman, who is the Hostess and owner of the restaurant. She has a French accent.

HOSTESS. Oh, Monsieur Au Briand, comment ca va?

O'BRIEN. Fine, merci.

HOSTESS. Did you 'ave a lovely day at the beach?

O'BRIEN. Yeah, yeah. My ex-wife won total custody of our kid today. I get to see him for two hours when he turns 12, and then again when he's 16.

HOSTESS. Oh, Monsieur, quelle dommage. Well, forget your troubles here on our beautiful island, and we at this restaurant will do all we can to soothe you.

O'BRIEN. Thank you. I'm feeling kind of gloomy.

HOSTESS. Oh, Monsieur. We lighten your troubles for you. Forget your wife, forget your child. You are in tropical paradise.

O'BRIEN. Yes, thank you. I am in paradise, right.

HOSTESS. Your usual table, Monsieur.

O'BRIEN. Yeah, I mean, oui.

HOSTESS. Oui, Monsieur. *(Guides him to his table; motions for him to sit:)* Si vous plait. *(O'Brien sits.)* Veronique will be your waitress tonight, Monsieur. Bon apetite.

O'BRIEN. Thank you. *(The Hostess goes away. After a moment, Kitty enters. She is very seductive, seductively dressed. She walks over to O'Brien's table, and then stands in front of him. Whenever she stands, she has a pronounced curve to her posture; she pushes her lower body forward. It seems seductive, but also a little weird. It should seem odd and explicit, but not like a contortion; her stance should be comfortable for her. It's just her pelvis pushes forward. Kitty is extremely flirtatious in her manner as well, in a very generalized way. She speaks in a French accent.)*

29

KITTY. Bonjour, Monsieur. My name is Kitty, I will be waitress ce soir.

O'BRIEN. I thought my waitress' name was Veronique.

KITTY. No, Monsieur. My name is Kitty. Je m'appelle Kitty, le chat d'amour.

O'BRIEN. Well, okay. Hiya, Kitty.

KITTY. Bonjour, Monsieur. *(She moves her lower body around in a circle, seductively.)* Would you like something to drink, Monsieur?

O'BRIEN. *(Responding to her flirtatiousness.)* A bottle of water. A bottle of wine. A hunk of cheese. Et vous, Mademoiselle.

KITTY. *(Laughs seductively.)* Et moi? Oh, no, Monsieur. Non, non, non. Kitty is not on ze menu.

O'BRIEN. Well, why are you standing that way then? Pull your private parts in. *(Kitty stands straight for a moment, pulling in her lower body so that her pelvis does not thrust forward. However, this posture is difficult to her. The "pelvis out" one is the one that feels natural to her. However, for now, she does her best to stand straight.)*

KITTY. Would you like to 'ear the specials, Monsieur?

O'BRIEN. Okay. Shoot.

KITTY. Tonight we 'ave filet of red snapper avec un sauce of artichokes et sardine. We 'ave Mahi Mahi avec un sauce de Mieu Mieu, in honor of ze French actress Mieu Mieu. The fish is flown in by aeroplane from ze island of Maui.

O'BRIEN. Mahi Mahi from Maui avec Mieu Mieu sauce.

KITTY. Oui, Monsieur. *(Unable to stand straight anymore, she reverts to her old posture, and lets her lower body thrust out again with relief; she explains seductively:)* I 'ave ze bad posture, Monsieur.

O'BRIEN. No, it's charming in its way. It's just I haven't had a woman in over a year. And your posture upsets me.

KITTY. *(Flirting.)* I do not know what you mean, Monsieur. *(Back to the specials.)* We 'ave mussels meuniere, we 'ave salade du Crab, we 'ave tuna grille avec Gerard Depardieu sauce; et finalement, we 'ave le specialité de la maison, le filet du soleil avec roast mouse et parakeet gratineé. Meow, meow, c'est une grande delicaceé. *(Shakes her lower body at him in ecstasy.)*

O'BRIEN. Kitty, please. I told you, I haven't had a woman in a year.

KITTY. Oui? Quelle dommage, Monsieur. Et what would you

like from ze menu zis evening?

O'BRIEN. Well, the specials sound interesting, especially that Maui Maui fish served with Muck Muck sauce. But what I would like is a good old American hamburger, cooked rare, with French fries and cole slaw. I hope you don't think badly of me by my order.

KITTY. Pas du tout, Monsieur. Kitty does not judge. Kitty loves all choices, she sees no difference between any of zem. But let me tell ze kitchen of your wishes. (*Screams out, a bit vulgar.*) Hey, Mario! Gimme a Number 42, with grease and slaw, bloody! (*Back to O'Brien; flirtatious and French again.*) Anything else, Monsieur, you wish from Kitty? (*She waves her lower body at him again.*)

O'BRIEN. Not right now. Thank you very much.

KITTY. Oui, Monsieur. (*Kitty walks away seductively, exits. A young Waiter, cute, comes on, holding a basket of bread. He comes over to O'Brien and, like Kitty, sticks out his lower body and waves it at him.*)

WAITER. (*Waving his lower body seductively; French accent.*) Would you like a basket of bread, Monsieur?

O'BRIEN. What?

WAITER. Basket, Monsieur? (*Waves his lower body with energy.*)

O'BRIEN. No, go away. I'm not interested. (*Waiter puts bread on table, walks away, annoyed or disappointed in the response; exits. To himself.*) What island am I on exactly, I wonder? (*Kitty appears R., across the stage from O'Brien. She holds a bottle of wine and a glass.*)

KITTY. I am bringing you ze wine, Monsieur. (*Kitty raises the bottle and the glass into the air. The Waiter comes back, next to Kitty, and begins to play the bongo drums. Kitty begins to dance towards O'Brien with the wine, but with very slow, samba-like movements, always leading with her lower body. It is a seductive, strange dance she is doing. Her dance does take her toward the table, but it will take a very, very long time for her to actually get to O'Brien if she keeps going at this slow, seductive, rhythmic speed. Kitty smiles delightedly while she does this dance, and keeps moving her hips and that pelvic area of hers.*)

O'BRIEN. (*Stares for quite a while; eventually becomes impatient.*) Faster, faster! I haven't got all day. (*The bongo rhythm goes much faster, and Kitty speeds up her dance movements and gets to his table much faster. The dance, sped up this way, looks much less sexy and much more peculiar, silly, an odd and unnecessary way to cross a room. Kitty arrives at the table. The Waiter finishes the bongos with a definitive thump, and exits.)*

KITTY.   Sometimes it takes a very long time to get across ze room.

O'BRIEN.   Ah yes. Does it? *(Kitty puts the wine glass on the table, and holds up the wine bottle.)*

KITTY.   Your wine, Monsieur. *(Kitty tries to pour the wine into the glass. However, the bottle is corked and nothing comes out of the bottle.)* It ees not coming out, Monsieur.

O'BRIEN.   Well, do you have a corkscrew?

KITTY.   *(Blushingly flirtatious.)* Oh, Monsieur ... a cork ... screw??? Oh, Monsieur, you make Kitty blush avec your obscenities. *(Laughing like a school child.)* Screw, screw? Oh, my, I am beside myself!

O'BRIEN.   *(Sort of annoyed.)* Do you have a corkscrew to open the wine?

KITTY.   *(Thinks; not flirtatious.)* No, I don't.

O'BRIEN.   Well, take it away then.

KITTY.   *(Calls offstage for Waiter.)* Gaston! *(The Waiter comes back and plays bongos again, so that Kitty can dance off with the wine. She dances away quickly this time. She and the Waiter exit R. Another waitress, Veronique, enters from L. She goes up to O'Brien's table.)*

VERONIQUE.   *(Speaks with an over-the-top Cockney accent.)* 'Allo there, guv'nor! I'm your waitress, Veronique. 'Ow would you like a nice plate of beef and Yorkshire pudding, eh, ducks? Or a lovely cheese and tomahto sandwhich. Or a lovely shepherd's pie?

O'BRIEN.   I'm sorry, your name is Veronique?

VERONIQUE.   That's me name. I live in a flat with me mom, underneath the loo at Victoria Station. I come 'ere in the tube, and in the mornings I eat digestive biscuits.

O'BRIEN.   I see. Kitty was waiting on me before.

VERONIQUE.   We don't 'ave no Kitty 'ere, sir.

O'BRIEN.   But she was just here. She did a dance to the bongo drums.

VERONIQUE.   Bongo drums. Blimey, sir ... your imagination

is runnin' away with you.

O'BRIEN. She was just here. She walks funny.

VERONIQUE. Uh huh. Whatever you say, guv.

O'BRIEN. Never mind. Do you have a corkscrew?

VERONIQUE. What for?

O'BRIEN. For a bottle of wine. Oh that's right, she took the wine away.

VERONIQUE. We don't serve wine 'ere, sir. 'ow about a lovely lager, or a bit o' ale, or a nice cup a' tea served with a delicious bit of digestive biscuit.

O'BRIEN. Never mind. I'll wait for Kitty.

VERONIQUE. You'll wait a long time then, guv'nor. *(Exits L.)*

O'BRIEN. *(Wanting Kitty; calling toward R. where she had exited.)* Oh, waitress! Oh, waitress! *(Veronique comes back on.)*

VERONIQUE. Yes?

O'BRIEN. No, I wanted Kitty.

VERONIQUE. *(Threatening a punishment.)* Do you want me to bring you your check?

O'BRIEN. Well, I haven't even eaten yet.

VERONIQUE. Then don't go on about Kitty please. Now you eat your bread and water, and if you're well be'aved, maybe Matron will reinstate your privileges.

O'BRIEN. What? Matron? Privileges? Am I in a play by Pirandello?

VERONIQUE. I'm sure I don't know, sir. *(Exits.)*

O'BRIEN. *(Calling, a bit softer.)* Kitty. Oh, Kitty. *(Veronique is back in, in a flash.)*

VERONIQUE. What did you say?

O'BRIEN. Nothing. I said absolutely nothing.

VERONIQUE. All right, then. *(Exits.)*

O'BRIEN. *(Waits a few seconds; then calls plaintively:)* Kitty ... oh, Kitty.... Here, Kitty, here, Kitty ... I miss you. Oh, Kitty ... *(Veronique comes back on, leading in the Hostess and pointing to O'Brien, indicating there is some issue. Veronique exits.)*

HOSTESS. Monsieur Au Briand, my apologies. Veronique has told me that the kitty was bothering you, I am so sorry.

O'BRIEN. What? No, no one was bothering me.

HOSTESS. I 'ave taken care that the kitty will bother you no more. We 'ave called up ze veterinarian, and 'e will put kitty to sleep momentarily.

O'BRIEN. Put her to sleep? I don't know what you mean.

HOSTESS.   Please, do not feel bad. Many other guests have objected to the cat before ... she rubs against the legs, they are allergic, she makes them sneeze. She makes the bus boys play the bongos. She has been warned; it is only right she be put to death.

O'BRIEN. Good God, where is the vet? I must stop this.

HOSTESS. But your dinner, Monsieur ....

O'BRIEN. I don't want her death on my conscience. My ex-wife can't be right about me. I don't destroy all women I meet, do I?

HOSTESS. I am sure I don't know, Monsieur.

O'BRIEN. The address of the veterinarian ... quickly, quickly!

HOSTESS. Soixante-cinq, rue du chat du mort.

O'BRIEN. Oh, God. (*O'Brien runs off. Lights change, and we are in another part of the stage. The Vet, in a white coat, is standing over Kitty, who is in a fur coat [maybe] and lying on a cot. The Vet has just finished giving Kitty a shot from a hypodermic.*)

VETERINARIAN. Bon nuit, Kitty.

O'BRIEN. Wait, wait ... don't give her a shot. She was my waitress. I loved her.

VETERINARIAN. Too late. Ze kitty kat is on her way. Au revoir, kitty kat. (*Exits. O'Brien kneels by Kitty's side.*)

O'BRIEN. Kitty, Kitty, I'm here, don't die.

KITTY. Good-bye, Monsieur. You did not love Kitty, and so the doctor, he give me a shot. It ees time to leave. I 'ave danced enough.

O'BRIEN. Oh, Kitty, no. I realize now. You're my reason for living.

KITTY. Oh, Monsieur, do not try to cheer up a dying kitty. I am past it. I 'ave 'ad a full life. I 'ave lapped ze milk. I 'ave arched ze back. I 'ave eaten ze mouse, I 'ave chased ze para-keet. It ees time for Kitty to move on.

O'BRIEN. No, I have nothing.

KITTY. We 'ave Paris, Monsieur.

O'BRIEN. We do? I don't remember anything about Paris.

KITTY. Well, zen we 'ave nothing, Monsieur. Oh, the sodium pentathal is working. Au revoir, au revoir, I am leaving ... life number ... 5, it is ending. Oh God, 4 more to go. So many disappointments, so many ze twists and ze turns. How difficile is la vie du chat. Oh ... oh ... c'est finie. *(Kitty dies. O'Brien moans in sorrow and bows his head. The Vet comes in and gives O'Brien a hypodermic shot of something. O'Brien cries out in pain and looks surprised.)*

O'BRIEN. Ow! What are you doing?

VETERINARIAN. I am sorry, Monsieur. My mind, it wandered. I did not mean to give you a shot. But it is too late. Good-bye. *(O'Brien looks shocked, then falls over dead. Vet shrugs, what can you do? Lights out. End.)*

PROPERTY LIST

Basket of bread (WAITER)
Bottle of wine (KITTY)
Wine glass (KITTY)
Bongo drums (WAITER)
Hypodermic needle (VETERINARIAN)

AUTHOR'S NOTE

Afterword

Since fall 1994, fellow playwright Marsha Norman and I have been chairing a Playwriting Program at the Juilliard School, Drama Division, in New York City. We team teach — that is, we run class literally together. (Marsha and I obviously have different writing styles, but personally we get on very well, and have discovered that our thoughts and opinions on plays and on writing have much in common.) It is a one year program, with a possible additional year residency fellowship for some of the students.

In 1996-97, we had seven students; and it was their idea to present an evening of short plays at Juilliard. Since with Marsha and me, that meant a total of nine writers, someone (or some combination of Alex Tolk, Hilary Bell and Marsha) came up with the idea of writing plays about the nine lives of a cat. There were no rules, except we should let a person play the cat and we should limit the length to about nine minutes or so. We otherwise did no planning to coordinate, and all wrote what we wrote.

My play was inspired by an actual waitress I encountered on the island of St. Barths in the Caribbean, who over several days kept flirting with a friend of mine. She had this very seductive posture (not good for curvature of the spine, I'm sure), where she tended to lean backwards slightly, in a relaxed stance, thus sort of "leading" with her lower body.

In terms of capturing this stance for the play, it's important that the stance be exaggerated, but not acrobatic, not like a gymnast about to flip over backwards. It is seductive, but it is also more or less comfortable for the actress, it's just it absolutely puts her pelvic area forward.

A few other tidbits of advice.

The accents are important. The actresses playing the Hostess and Kitty should be very comfortable with French accents and French pronunciations. Not only are there many French words and phrases in their dialogue, but there are also many English words they say that should nonetheless be said with French emphases (such as "restaurant," "Crab" with an Ah sound, "parakeet"). I think it would be wise not to cast anyone who wasn't already knowledgeable about French pronunciation; but if you do, have someone handy to coach them well.

Similarly, Veronique's Cockney accent should also be a strong one (though I think that accent is easier to fake). Please, though, have the Cockney Veronique say her name with the right, proper French pronunciation. Don't make a joke that she says her name as Veron-ick; the joke is that she has a legitimate French name (Veron-neek), but is otherwise seemingly smack dab in the middle of Picadilly Circus.

When Kitty momentarily loses her French accent to call out Mr. O'Brien's hamburger order to the kitchen, don't get hung up wondering whether Kitty is only pretending to be French. She is French; I have her drop it for that moment alone for a joke — as if anytime you call to a kitchen it's in that loud, crass American way. (Or maybe it's his hamburger order that makes her make that transition.) But don't get stuck thinking it means more than it does.

Obviously, the play was written to fit into an evening of "cat" plays. (And thus Kitty's reference to "life number five" being over had more resonance when the play was fifth in the evening.) However, having just had the play done on its own this past summer, I think the play can also work on its own terms: a comedy about a ridiculously flirtatious waitress that then turns into a comic, bizarre fantasy where the waitress, it turns out, is also a cat.

I had a lot of fun writing this play; and the two times it's been done so far, it seems to go really well with the audience. If you choose to do it, I hope you have fun too.

FUNERAL PARLOR

FUNERAL PARLOR was included in the ABC TV special CAROL, CARL, WHOOPI AND ROBIN, which originally aired February 2, 1987 (Marcy Carsey and Tom Werner, Executive Producers; Stephanie Sills, Dick Clair and Jenna McMahon, Producers). Writing was supervised by Dick Clair and Jenna McMahon. It was directed by Harvey Korman and Roger Beatty and written by Chris Durang, Jim Evering, Ken Welch, Mitzi Welch, Dick Clair and Jenna McMahon. Musical material was by Ken Welch and Mitzi Welch. The cast was as follows:

SUSAN ....Carol Burnett
MARCUS ....Robin Williams

Subsequently, the sketch was part of A MESS OF PLAYS BY CHRIS DURANG at South Coast Repertory, with Jodi Thelen as SUSAN and Howard Shangraw as MARCUS. And as part of MIX AND MATCH DURANG at the John Drew Theatre, with Claire Lautier as SUSAN and Michael Ian Black as MARCUS.

CHARACTERS

SUSAN, the widow
MARCUS, a visitor at the funeral

FUNERAL PARLOR

Scene: A funeral parlor. A closed casket, lots of flowers, very quiet, hushed.

Susan, the widow, is dressed in black, with pearls. She is sedate, proper, formal.

A few people are in line, offering their condolences, shaking her hand. She acknowledges them with a little nod and a little smile, and a whispered "thank you."

About to reach Susan in line is a man named Marcus. Marcus is dressed in a nice suit, but it's kind of a light color, and his tie and shirt are kind of flowery, not really right for a funeral, but maybe he had to come straight from work (or Hawaii). Otherwise he looks appropriate enough.

The person ahead of Marcus makes quiet sounds of condolences and leaves. Marcus reaches Susan. He is sincere and genuine, it's just that he's, well, odd.

[Note: the other mourners can be mimed or dispensed with, if you choose.]

MARCUS. Susan, I'm so sorry. My deepest condolences.
SUSAN. Yes, thank you ... (??) *(She doesn't know who Marcus is.)*
MARCUS. Marcus.
SUSAN. *(Still doesn't know him, but is gracious.)* Yes, Marcus. Thank you for coming.
MARCUS. We'll all miss him terribly.
SUSAN. Yes. It's a great loss.
MARCUS. We'll all miss him.
SUSAN. Yes.
MARCUS. You must feel terrible.

SUSAN.   Well ... I don't feel good. It was a terrible shock.

MARCUS.   Death is always a shock. You're sitting home doing nothing, and then suddenly death goes "Boo!", and somebody falls down dead.

SUSAN.   Yes. *(Looks around, hopes someone else will come over.)*

MARCUS.   What were his last words? Were they "boo?"

SUSAN.   What? "Boo?" No. He didn't really have any last words.

MARCUS.   Did he make any last noises?

SUSAN.   Noises? What?

MARCUS.   Guttural sorts of noises? Or high pitched shrieking ones? *(Makes high pitched sounds:)* Eeeeeeeek! Eeeeeeeeek! Awooooga! Awooooooga!

SUSAN.   Just noises, I don't know. They were lower than that. Don't do that anymore.

MARCUS.   *(Sympathetically.)* Oh, Susan, you poor, poor thing. *(Turns to someone who's gotten in line behind him.)* I wouldn't wait if I were you, I'm going to be a while. *(The person in line looks surprised but goes away; Susan looks alarmed.)* All alone in the house now. Alone in the kitchen. Alone in the dining room. Alone in the living room — living room, that's a mocking phrase now, isn't it? Alone, alone, alone. All alone. Alone, alone, alone.

SUSAN.   Please don't go on.

MARCUS.   Yes, but you have to mourn, Susan, to *mourn*. I always thought the Irish were right to do all that keening. Do you want to keen, Susan?

SUSAN.   Not really. Thank you anyway.

MARCUS.   How about singing a Negro spiritual?

SUSAN.   I don't think so. *(Looks about madly for people.)*

MARCUS.   *(Sings.)*

Swing low, sweet chariot,
Comin' for to carry me home ...

SUSAN.   Thank you for coming.

MARCUS.   Don't you want to sing?

SUSAN.   I don't want to keen or sing. I'm an Episcopalian. I'll cry quietly in my room later this evening. Now I must attend to the other mourners.

MARCUS. Susan, you're avoiding the sadness, I can't let you do that.

SUSAN. Please, please let me do that. It's been a terrible day. I have to bury my husband.

MARCUS. Is he in the casket? It's a closed casket, he's not actually in some other room, propped up in some stuffed chair or other, waiting there to startle someone, is he?

SUSAN. Certainly not. Thank you so much for coming.

MARCUS. That would give someone quite a fright. They'd be standing by this chair making conversation and then realize they were talking to him, only he was stark, stone dead! Ahahahahaha, that would be a good one!

SUSAN. Yes, very good. *(Calls.)* Oh, David! *(No luck.)*

MARCUS. I'm going to miss him too, you know.

SUSAN. Ah, how nice. Or rather, how sad. Well, time heals everything.

MARCUS. You're not the only one with sorrow written on your forehead.

SUSAN. What?

MARCUS. I should say not. *(Shows his forehead, previously covered with bangs; it has "sorrow" written on it.)* Magic marker. Doesn't wash off. We're going to miss him on the commuter train. We used to exchange morning pleasantries. "Nice morning," or "Cold enough for you?" or "The train seems to be on time today for a change."

SUSAN. I see. Excuse me, I think the mortician is signaling me.

MARCUS. You know, your husband was the only person on that whole damn train who was even willing to speak to me.

SUSAN. *(Very much at a loss.)* How interesting.

MARCUS. The other people would get panic in their eyes if I even started to walk in their direction, and they'd move away, or pretend to be sleeping. But they didn't fool me, I'm no dope, YOU CAN'T SLEEP *STANDING UP!*

SUSAN. Well, if you're tired enough maybe you can.

MARCUS. Your husband, though, was always very friendly to me. Not like my father. Nowadays my father won't even return my phone calls, I went to a seance and everything.

45

SUSAN. What?

MARCUS. Well he's dead, but I have this medium friend who gave me this special 800 number that lets you call the dead. Maybe you'd like the number to try to reach your husband on the other side.

SUSAN. I don't think so. Well, que sera, sera. Ah me. Lah dee dah. Well thank you so much for coming.

MARCUS. *(Warmly.)* Well, you're welcome. I just feel so terrible about your husband being gone, and I don't know what I'm going to do on the train in the morning.

SUSAN. Yes. Well — why don't you read a book?

MARCUS. That's an idea. Do you have any suggestions?

SUSAN. Oh my, I don't know. *The Thorn Birds, Great Expectations.* Any book, I don't care.

MARCUS. My favorite book is *Babar the Elephant.*

SUSAN. Yes, that is excellent.

MARCUS. Have you read it?

SUSAN. No, but I hear wonderful things. Ah me. My, my. Well, thank you for coming. Good-bye.

MARCUS. *(Surprised.)* Are you leaving?

SUSAN. *(Losing her temper.)* No, I'm not leaving. I want *you* to leave. You're making me hysterical. Can't you take a hint? When I say "Thank you for coming," that's code for "Go away now." Don't you understand that?

MARCUS. *(Terribly abashed, a bit hurt.)* Oh. I'm sorry. I thought it just meant "thank you for coming." I'm sorry. I didn't realize. I ... Is there anything else you've said in code I haven't understood?

SUSAN. No. Nothing. I don't think so.

MARCUS. *(Still a little thrown.)* Oh good. *(He looks very abashed and embarrassed.)*

SUSAN. It's ...just ... well ... *(Feeling badly for him.)* Oh dear, now I feel terribly guilty about having expressed my emotions.

MARCUS. *(Friendly again, thinking of her.)* Oh don't feel guilty about expressing emotions. That's a *good* thing to do. You've had a terrible loss.

SUSAN. *(Somewhat seriously, realizing.)* Yes, I have.

MARCUS. Are you sure you don't want to keen yet? I'm not

Irish, but I think it's a very appropriate thing to do at a wake.

SUSAN.   Oh I don't know. Maybe another time.

MARCUS.   This would be the most likely time.

SUSAN.   Well, I don't know. *(A little interested.)* What does keening sound like exactly?

MARCUS.   Oh, it's real interesting. It's sort of like this. *(Marcus makes an enormously strange, low, sustained moan-whine that goes up and down the scale. Eventually it has real emotion in it. The rest of the people present come to a dead halt and stare.)*

SUSAN.   *(To crowd; slightly annoyed.)* Please, stop staring. Go back to your conversational buzz. *(The crowd goes back to its hum.)*

MARCUS.   Did I do something wrong again?

SUSAN.   Well, it was a very startling sound.

MARCUS.   It's just like crying, but more dramatic. I love to cry. You loved your husband, didn't you?

SUSAN.   *(Genuine.)* Yes.

MARCUS.   Well, then, don't you want to keen just a little?

SUSAN.   Well, I see your point a little but ... I don't know that I really could.

MARCUS.   You could do it softer than I did.

SUSAN.   I don't think so.

MARCUS.   Oh please, I'm sure it would make you feel better.

SUSAN.   *(Wanting to feel better.)* Would it? *(Starts to, but freezes.)* Ohhhhh ... *(Stops.)* This is difficult to do in public. Couldn't I call you later this evening, and do it on the phone?

MARCUS.   No, it's much more healing to keen at the funeral. You shouldn't do it on the phone.

SUSAN.   Oh, I don't know.

MARCUS.   Come on. It'll help.

SUSAN.   *(Hesitates, but then.)* Oooooooo. *(It's very soft. Sounds like a ghost sound, or a person imitating the wind.)*

MARCUS.   That's good.

SUSAN.   Oooooooo.

MARCUS.   That's good.

SUSAN.   Oooooooo.

MARCUS.   That's good. AAAAAAOOOOWWWWWOOOOO-OOOOOOOO!!!! *(Lets loose with very full-out keening sounds. Susan looks aghast for a moment. The crowd stops and stares again. After a beat, Susan gives in to some odd combination of grief and having fun, and makes extremely loud keening sounds simultaneously with Marcus.)*

BOTH.   AAAAAAAAAAOOOOOOOOOOOOOOOOWWWWWWW-OOOOOOOOOOOOOOOOOOOOOOOOOOOOOOOOOOOOOOOO OO!!!!!! *(From out of these very satisfying, if shocking, noises, Susan starts to cry loudly and uninhibitedly. Marcus pats her on the back in a comforting manner, looking out at the crowd a bit proudly as if to say "See what I did?" Susan's crying subsides, and her breathing returns more to normal.)*

MARCUS.   There, that's better.

SUSAN.   *(Drying her eyes.)* Thank you so much for coming. *(Just as Marcus begins to wonder what she means.)* No, no, not code. Thank you. I feel much better.

MARCUS.   Oh good. Well, you're welcome. *(Marcus and Susan shake hands warmly. Marcus smiles at her, moves aside, as other mourners come over to speak to Susan. Lights fade.)*

AUTHOR'S NOTE

This is a sketch that was part of a Carol Burnett TV special, CAROL, CARL, WHOOPI AND ROBIN, that aired on ABC in 1987.

I'm a fan of Carol Burnett and so was excited when I was asked to submit a sketch for this special. My original sketch was between two women; I envisioned the crazy mourner as a nutty part for Carol.

From the sketch, I was asked to come work for four weeks in LA as a staff writer for the special, under the head writers, Dick Clair and Jenna McMahon. Dick and Jenna had written many of Carol's funniest sketches for years, including all the ones about Eunice and her mother fighting on and on and on.

Once I was on staff, I learned that Carol actually didn't want to play the crazy part, she was more interested in playing the "normative" role, the reactor role. And on learning that Robin Williams was to be a guest star, changing the mourner to a man seemed a natural.

The special was filmed three times — the rehearsal, and two run-throughs, all in front of audience.

The first two times Robin did the sketch more or less as written and rehearsed, but he made it clear that he wanted to try a wilder version where he could ad-lib further crazy comments. So Carol announced to the audience on the last run-through that Robin was going to pull stuff out of his hat, "I have no idea what he's going to do, and so I figure ... let 'im." Then she added, "pray for me."

Robin's ad-lib version was quite funny, though the "story" of the sketch no longer really registered. (And Carol had wanted the sketch to have a "point," she wanted the crazy man to actually have a positive effect on the woman in the long run.)

When I saw the first edit a couple of months later, I was distressed by what had happened. They had edited the three takes together, so that sometimes Robin seemed to be playing a part, and Carol was reacting to what he was doing as that character; and sometimes he'd be riffing, and Carol would actually be playing reactions to Robin himself and his free-associating, not to the character he was playing. (And Robin sometimes seemed a character, and sometimes seemed himself.)

Sense of my own authorial propriety aside, I found the sketch schizoid and confusing when edited that way. I preferred that they either keep to the versions where he played the material as written, or go to the other extreme and just show all of his ad-libbing one.

But wonder of wonders, fate sort of gave me the best solution. There was another sketch in the evening that was just not working as they edited it together (which was a shame; it was funny when they worked on it). And so suddenly they had a whole 10 minute section to fill in the special.

And the solution they came up with was to first show the full version of my sketch with Robin staying in character; and then to follow it with his own ad-libbed version in its entirety — and his ad-libbed version was much funnier when you knew what he was riffing on top of.

So I was delighted with this result; and Robin won an Emmy actually.

The version published here is my version of the sketch. (To see Robin's riff version of it, watch for the repeat of the special. It seems to show up on the Disney channel with some regularity.)

TO THE ACTORS: The most important thing about the sketch is that Marcus is well intentioned, he is not meant to be being mean. He's like a hyper-active child grown-up, he doesn't have a good sense of what's appropriate or not. But he's good-hearted like a child too.

And don't be intimidated by the fame of the two actors who originated the parts — find your own sense of what fits your own persona, particularly with the part of Marcus. Marcus' "sincerity" can be played in different ways; Robin's high energy, brain-racing persona fit the sketch very well, but the character can be emotionally colored in other ways too. Just be truthful to yourself, and come from a place of trying to help Susan, but just not having a good sense of how to behave in public.

The part of Susan is easier, but very important: simple, genuine, good at listening. How she "hears" the strange things Marcus says and reacts to them — sometimes with a covered politeness, sometimes with alarm, sometimes with disapproval and dread — this "hearing" she does needs to be there for the scene to happen and for the comedy to register.

CANKER SORES AND OTHER DISTRACTIONS

AUTHOR'S NOTE

This is another sketch I wrote with Carol Burnett in mind. I thought she could be the difficult waitress Midge.

However, it's never been done. And I found it in my trunk (or rather on my computer, which sometimes is like a trunk).

CHARACTERS

MARTIN
PRUNELLA, his ex-wife
MIDGE, a waitress

man, I always have loved this

CANKER SORES AND OTHER DISTRACTIONS

Scene: A restaurant.

Martin and Prunella, a well-dressed couple.

MARTIN.   Prunella, it's so good to see you.

PRUNELLA.   You too, Martin.

MARTIN.   Prunella, how I've missed saying your name. Prunella, Prunella, Prunella. Like prunes with vanilla.

PRUNELLA.   Martin, Martin. I ... can't think of anything equivalent to say.

MARTIN.   How long has it been?

PRUNELLA.   It's been a long time.

MARTIN.   It's been a long time, hasn't it, Prunella. Prunella, Prunella.

PRUNELLA.   Ten years. Ever since our divorce.

MARTIN.   That dreadful day. We had a particularly contentious divorce too, didn't we? Swearing, crying, hurling accusations. I said so many awful things. You said so many awful things. Then you got all our possessions and the house and the kids and the car.

PRUNELLA.   I know. We really hated one another back then. As a matter of fact, we've continued hating one another until ... just yesterday, that chance meeting on the street.

MARTIN.   It's true, Prunella. When I saw you yesterday, the sunlight shimmering on your wig, all of a sudden all the hate and anger fell into perspective, and I thought, I love this woman, I always have loved this woman. I mean, who cares who got what in the settlement — those are only "things."

PRUNELLA.   Yes. *My* things.

MARTIN.   Right, but the point is, Prunella, after ten years of hating you, suddenly that hate has lifted and in its place is well,

57

it's corny to say it, but in its place is love.

PRUNELLA. I feel the same way, Martin. The kids are grown, the car is broken, the house needs repair. But our love for one another is real.

MARTIN. Prunella, I know this is crazy, and the last thing either of us thought would ever happen, but I think we should get back together. I want us to remarry. *(A rather unwilling waitress named Midge approaches their table. She's not hostile, it's just there are about 20 other places she would rather be.)*

MIDGE. Hello, my name is Midge, and I will be your waitress for the evening. Let me tell you about our specials, and then take a cocktail order.

MARTIN. Could you come back in a minute?

MIDGE. What?

MARTIN. I'm sorry. Would you come back in a minute. I was in the middle of a thought. *(Midge thinks and mutters to herself, and sort of sluffs away.)* Now where was I?

PRUNELLA. Oh, Martin, it's amazing you feel this way because I feel absolutely the same.

MARTIN. You do?

PRUNELLA. Yes. I haven't felt anything like ...

MIDGE. *(Trying again.)* We got duck and chicken and fish, all almondine.

MARTIN. I'm not ready now.

MIDGE. *(By rote; as if repetition will make this work out.)* My name is Midge, and I'm your waitress.

MARTIN. My name is Martin, and I'm not ready yet.

MIDGE. Well, when you're ready you let me know. Okay?

MARTIN. Yes, Midge.

MIDGE. I'll be waiting. *(Walks away.)*

MARTIN. Now what were you saying?

PRUNELLA. I forget.

MARTIN. Oh I hate it when this happens. Well, let me tell you more about my feelings then. Stop me if you've heard it before. I feel so thoroughly renewed, young, in love ... I ... *(Suddenly realizing.)* I think I'm developing a canker sore.

PRUNELLA. What?

MARTIN. Yes, right on my inner cheek. *(Puts his tongue there.)*

Ow, it hurts when I put my tongue on it.

PRUNELLA. Don't put your tongue on it then.

MARTIN. I have to. It hurts.

PRUNELLA. When did you get it, darling?

MARTIN. *(Cranky.)* I don't know, I don't know, it just happened.

PRUNELLA. Darling, I'm sorry.

MIDGE. *(Holding a tray of five drinks.)* Did you all order drinks?

MARTIN. No we didn't.

MIDGE. Well somebody did. I wonder who it was. *(She puts the drinks down on their table, and looks through her notes.)* No ... no ... no ...

PRUNELLA. *(To Martin.)* Go on, dear, I'm listening.

MARTIN. *(In pain, grouchy.)* I was saying I feel so alive, so renewed ... damn it, Prunella, this canker sore is just hurting, it's sitting in my mouth and it's hurting me.

PRUNELLA. Maybe you could drink something. *(To Midge.)* Is there any drink you could recommend that makes a canker sore feel better?

MIDGE. Grapefruit juice.

MARTIN. Better, not worse!

MIDGE. I'm not sure if we have grapefruit juice. We have Mimosas, but somebody said the orange juice tasted like grapefruit juice. I'll go check. *(Leaves her pad on the table and exits.)*

PRUNELLA. Don't forget your pad.

MARTIN. I don't want grapefruit juice, Midge.

MIDGE. *(From offstage.)* I'll check.

MARTIN. I'm becoming very sorry we've come to this restaurant.

PRUNELLA. Now, Martin, don't let it ruin this evening for us.

MARTIN. Are you telling me what to do already?

PRUNELLA. It's just a suggestion, don't be angry.

MARTIN. *(Angry.)* I'm not angry. I'm just coping with a canker sore.

PRUNELLA. More like a "cranker" sore.

MARTIN. What?

PRUNELLA. Canker and cranky sound alike. I was just noticing.

MARTIN. Canker and cranky. They don't sound particularly alike.

PRUNELLA. "Anker" and "anky." Well, they're more alike than, say, "canker" and "geranium."

MARTIN. This is becoming a stupid conversation.

PRUNELLA. Well, I'm sorry I brought it up. *(Silence for a moment.)*

MARTIN. *(Puts tongue in his cheek again.)* This really hurts.

PRUNELLA. Don't keep feeling it then.

MARTIN. It's hard not to.

PRUNELLA. Well, suit yourself. *(Pause.)* So you think we should get married again.

MARTIN. What? *(Distracted.)* Oh yes. I do. *(Midge comes back.)*

MIDGE. Did I leave my pad here? *(Picks it up.)* I don't know how you expect me to remember anything if I lose my pad.

MARTIN. We don't expect anything from you. Except service.

MIDGE. Well that's expecting something. *(Takes her pad and leaves.)*

PRUNELLA. Martin, we're getting distracted, and letting petty things interrupt our wonderful reconciliation. Let's not do that. Oh, oh, oh. *(Blinks her eye madly, throws her head back.)*

MARTIN. What is it?

PRUNELLA. Something in my eye. Oh dear. Oh my, it stings dreadfully. *(Prunella dabs her napkin in her glass of water and dabs her eye madly.)* Oh my. Ow. Ow.

MARTIN. I don't understand. Something just flew into your eye?

PRUNELLA. Well I'm not making it up. Ow ow ow. Oh dear. Ow.

MARTIN. Must you say ow? It sounds peculiar.

PRUNELLA. Well it hurts. Ow.

MARTIN. I believe it hurts. It just seems peculiar to have to be vocal about it.

PRUNELLA. Ow.

MARTIN. Seems unnecessary.

PRUNELLA. Don't try to control my pain. It's my pain. *(Midge comes back.)*

MIDGE. Here's your grapefruit juice.

PRUNELLA. Ow, ow.

MARTIN. I didn't order grapefruit juice.

MIDGE. Well I wrote it down. *(Shows him her pad.)*

MARTIN. I don't care what you wrote down, I don't want it.

MIDGE. Do you want a mimosa?

PRUNELLA. Ow, ow. Do you have an eye cup?

MIDGE. What?

PRUNELLA. To rinse my eye.

MIDGE. I can get a shot glass.

PRUNELLA. Yes. Please. Ow ow. *(Midge goes off to the bar.)*

MARTIN. Well my canker sore hurts too. *(To her, sort of.)* Ow. Especially when I touch it. Ow ow ow.

PRUNELLA. It's not a contest, Martin.

MARTIN. You always get this way when there are difficulties.

PRUNELLA. It's called appropriate response, Martin. My eye hurts. *(Midge comes back with the shot glass.)*

MIDGE. Here's the shot glass.

MARTIN. I don't want to get married again. It was a stupid idea. Life is nothing but pain and misery, it's stupid to have even thought about trying to look for something to work out.

PRUNELLA. Martin, you're overreacting. Eventually I'll get the thing out of my eye, and eventually your canker sore will leave.

MARTIN. It doesn't matter, something else awful will happen.

PRUNELLA. *(Still holding a napkin to her eye.)* Well, fine. I'm remembering what being married to you was like.

MIDGE. Oh, he's right. You get your hopes up and something awful happens. I got a call last week from representatives of Ed McMahon, and they said I won a million dollars. And then I thought, I'm going to quit my job as a waitress. But I misheard them. They said I *might* win a million dollars, if I agreed to subscribe to some magazine. So I ordered *TV Guide* for 36 weeks. And then last night my apartment got robbed, and I don't have a TV anymore. But I'm going to get *TV Guide* for 36 weeks.

MARTIN. Well that's too bad. I wonder if you could not talk to us so much this evening.

MIDGE. What?

PRUNELLA. Martin ...

MARTIN. Well, I didn't realize when I came in here that this was one of those talky-chatty restaurants.

MIDGE. What?

MARTIN. I would like to have a conversation with my ex-wife, but with you I would like to say hello and good-bye, and here's my order please.

MIDGE. Oh, you'd like to order now. *(To Prunella.)* He's difficult to understand.

MARTIN. I am not difficult to understand. I would like some politeness and decorum with the people whose work it is to serve me.

PRUNELLA. Just the check, please.

MIDGE. What?

PRUNELLA. Martin, I remembered why I divorced you. You're really horrible. You should be in therapy.

MIDGE. I'd love to be in therapy, but I can't afford it.

MARTIN. Where's the manager? I want this woman fired.

PRUNELLA. Just bring him the check. I'm going to go to a fast food restaurant. *(Leaves, holding her eye.)*

MARTIN. Where's the manager please?

MIDGE. I don't know if we have a manager. You want to see the cook?

MARTIN. Oh, forget it, forget it. Life is hopeless. You've ruined my remarriage. *(Stalks off.)*

MIDGE. Yeah, yeah. Big deal.

PROPERTY LIST

Tray with 5 drinks (MIDGE)
Notes pad (MIDGE)
Shot glass (MIDGE)
Napkin (PRUNELLA)

WOMAN STAND-UP

WOMAN STAND-UP was part of URBAN BLIGHT, which premiered at the Manhattan Theatre Club (Lynn Meadow, Artistic Director; Barry Grove, Managing Director) in New York City, on May 18, 1988. Based on an idea by John Tillinger, the evening was directed by Mr. Tillinger and Richard Maltby, Jr.; with music by David Shire, lyrics by Mr. Maltby, Jr., with an additional song by Edward Kleban. The twenty authors who had sketches in the evening were John Augustine, John Bishop, Christopher Durang, Jules Feiffer, Charles Fuller, Janusz Glowacki, A. R. Gurney, Jr., Tina Howe, E. Katherine Kerr, David Mamet, Terrence McNally, Arthur Miller, Reinaldo Povod, Jonathan Reynolds, Shel Silverstein, Ted Tally, Wendy Wasserstein, Richard Wesley, August Wilson, and George C. Wolfe. The set designs were by Heidi Landesman; the costume designs were by C. L. Hundley; and the lighting design was by Natasha Katz. URBAN BLIGHT was performed by a company of seven actors: Larry Fishburne, Nancy Giles, E. Katherine Kerr, Oliver Platt, Faith Prince, Rex Robbins, John Rubinstein.

WOMAN ....Faith Prince

Subsequently, this sketch was part of A MESS OF PLAYS BY CHRIS DURANG at South Coast Repertory, with Jodi Thelen as the WOMAN STAND-UP.

CHARACTERS

WOMAN, trying to be a stand-up

WOMAN STAND-UP

Scene: A comedy club. A Young Woman crosses to a microphone and speaks. She looks sweet and a bit frightened.

WOMAN. Hi, and welcome to the Comedy Club, New York's premiere comedy spot. My name is Cindy, and I am a stand-up comedienne.

Let me tell you about myself. I am fat, I am unmarried, I have roaches in my kitchen, I use feminine hygiene spray on my hair, and I have such low self-esteem that when my mother told me to get a nose job, I bought a Pit Bull and had it bite my nose off. *(There is the sound of recorded laughter over the sound system. The Woman smiles.)*

That's my laugh track.

Don't you just love Joan Rivers? Don't you just love her on Hollywood Squares? Don't you just love the tragedy behind Hollywood Squares? Joan Rivers' husband kills himself, Paul Lynde was a closeted homosexual and had a heart attack while doing poppers — I can't prove that, that's just hearsay, so please don't sue me — and John Davidson uses feminine hygiene spray on his dimples. But I sure do like that show. *(Laughs.)*

Don't you just love New York? Don't you love the rats in the sewers? Don't you love the beggars on the street while you go looking to buy a co-op? It's so much contrast everywhere, it makes my head spin. My head is on a washer-dryer cycle, every morning I hook my brain up to the sink and I wash it out for 15 minutes. This is my form of meditation. My brain is very clean, and it's very damaged.

I think I'd like the sound of a laugh track again please. *(The laugh track is played on the sound system again.)*

Thank you. Tell me, do you find me funny or do you find me disturbing?

My mother said to me, Cindy, don't give away your pussy to any man unless you marry him; you're worthless so don't give away your one claim to fame. And then on my first date with Teddy, I learned he was allergic to cats, so I got rid of my pussy. But now we have nothing to do on our honeymoon, so we played Pictionary and he went out with prostitutes. Could I have the laugh track again please? *(The laugh tracks plays again.)*

Thank you. I'm a stand-up comedienne, but I'm too insecure to go anywhere without my laugh track. My mother says I'm not only worthless, but I'm not funny. I wish my mother would die, then I'd have everybody over for brunch and serve Bloody Mary's made with her blood.

I'm sorry, that's not really funny, is it? It's New York, you see, I'm not well, all the suffering and the tension and the years of abuse, mental as well as physical that I received at the hands of my parents, has made me not fit to be a comedienne, but what else can I do with my life?

I went to a party the other day, and all the men in the room were homosexual. My mother says I am the cause of homosexuality in New York. So I said to her, okay, then I'm responsible for a lot of art and good musical comedies, and she said to me, no, you're just responsible for homosexuality. And for the dropping off in the birthrate because no man in his right mind could possibly like you. *(Cries briefly.)*

Do you understand why I have low self-esteem, or do you think I should tell more jokes like Joan Rivers? Laugh track, please. *(The laugh tracks plays.)*

Joan Rivers got fired from the Fox network. All she ever talks about is "grow up," "how big is your ring," and how she's so ugly. Why do people think she's funny? I'm much funnier, and I'm not even trying. *(The laugh track plays. Woman looks surprised.)*

I didn't ask for the laugh track, but thank you.

Don't you just love living in New York? I was in the subway the other day and everybody was covered with blood and was screaming. It was on the E train, and that's usually one of the nicer trains.

Then they took us all to the emergency room at B. Dalton, and Joan Collins was autographing one of her books. The clerks covered the dying people with gauze, and then Joan Collins took the gauze off the dying people and put it on the camera lens so she could look younger. I think she looks fine if you like a 50-year-old whore with a face lift. I'm sorry, I don't mean to be catty about other women, it's just that I have low self-esteem and I'm afraid to criticize men. *(The laugh track plays.)*

Well, I think it's time for me to go now. *(The laugh track plays again. Woman looks a bit confused, disoriented, sad.)*

Living in New York is really like living in hell, but in hell at least you know there's a heaven somewhere, but when you live in New York, there's only Newark and Trenton to think about. New Brunswick probably isn't bad. Maybe I could marry some professor from Rutgers ... but no, I forgot, I'm hideous and worthless.

Well, I apologize for taking up your time. You've been a great audience, well, not great, but not totally worthless like me. There must be a better way to live, but I don't know what it is! But if you see me in the gutter and I'm starving, I hope you'll give me a nickel! Good night! *(She waves good-bye. The sound of the laugh track, the sound of canned applause.)*

AUTHOR'S NOTE

Afterword

This is a strange piece, and I quite like it. My idea was to make use of all the jokey self-deprecations that are in a lot of women stand-up acts (like Joan Rivers, always talking about what a "dog" she is, or women talking about their weight), and to make those attempts at jokey self-deprecation come out of the mouth of a truly vulnerable, wounded young woman who has obviously been damaged by all the awful things her mother (and others) have said to her. Thus we are meant to believe what this young woman says. She has a *truly* damaged self-image. The conceit of the piece is that she's trying to turn the pain and emotional abuse of her life into comedy, but she isn't succeeding. Thus it "sounds" like comic stand-up, but it's not working ... her vulnerability is too clear.

I wrote the sketch for a multi-authored musical revue about city life called URBAN BLIGHT, which was produced by the Manhattan Theatre Club in 1988.

Since this is a monologue, I was very anxious during the casting to find out who would do the piece. Director John Tillinger told me they found this talented woman who really made the piece work in auditions, and her name was Faith Prince. And when I saw her, she was wonderful — she played the part as inwardly wounded, she was clearly telling the truth about what her mother said to her, she had the proper sound of someone trying to imitate the rhythms of stand-up comedy she had heard, but she kept looking uncertain, panicked. She was the walking wounded, though played by an actress with a comic gift, so it didn't just get serious.

Faith was a stand-out in the other authors' material in the evening as well, and it's been fun to follow her upward rise since then: a Tony nomination for JEROME ROBBINS' BROADWAY, stopping the show in a supporting part in NICK AND NORA, and then winning all the awards (including the Tony) for her Miss Adelaide in the hit revival of GUYS AND DOLLS. But the first time I saw her was doing this piece, WOMAN STAND-UP.

To the Actor

The key to making this piece work seems to be to cast an actress who is innately vulnerable. She then must play that the awful things that her mother has said to her — which she tells in the form of conventional, stand-up comedy rhythms — are truly what her mother has said to her. And so, even though she's trying to fit into the world of stand-up comedy, she's still upset by believing the dreadful put-downs she's grown up with. So it's a strange piece ... it is funny, but it's uncomfortable.

When an actress only plays the rhythm and sounds of stand-up, the piece literally doesn't work.

If the portrayal is only about capturing a stand-up comedy style (copying the delivery rhythms of, say, Joan Rivers or Elayne Boosler or Rosie O'Donnell) — but with no undercurrent of vulnerability and pain — then the piece appears to be about a brash young woman who has a failed comedy act; the audience thinks the point is that they're supposed to find it funny that her jokes fail.

When this happens, this is painful for me, because the piece isn't written to function that way. Yes, her act fails, but it's not the failure of a brash, loud, *confident* young woman who just doesn't have good material; it's meant to be the failure of an insecure, extremely non-confident woman, and her material, good or bad, has grown directly out of her psyche, it's not just that she came across some bad joke writing.

Her vulnerability and pain have collided with the sounds of self-deprecating humor that is in some stand-up, and it combines to create a very strange mixture. (If Elayne Boosler or Joan Rivers put themselves down, I never for a minute actually worry about them; we should worry about this woman.)

Aside from Faith Prince (who you may not know if you haven't seen her on Broadway), think of the sensitive souls of actresses like Julie Hagerty or Dianne Wiest (especially in PARENTHOOD) or young Judy Holliday (especially in ADAM'S RIB), and imagine them doing the piece, and then you'll have an idea of how to approach it.

I also saw the piece done in showcase by a young woman named Margaret Inoue, who seemed like a young Marilyn Monroe, in terms of prettiness and spaciness; her pain was not as clear as Faith's, but it was replaced, effectively, by a cloudiness that Marilyn used to have, as if she was almost medicated. This also worked — it wasn't that she was druggy, it was as if she lived under a psychological cloud that protected her from knowing what she was really feeling; when she would smile seductively, in a generalized way, after what she thought was a punch line, you thought: this woman is out to lunch; something's happened to her; what was it? So that was another interpretation that I thought worked.

But not brash, not confident. Vulnerable, trying to sound like a stand-up comic, but not succeeding too well. (After all, she's brought her own laugh track out of insecurity.)

DMV TYRANT

DMV TYRANT was part of URBAN BLIGHT at the Manhattan Theatre Club (Lynn Meadow, Artistic Director; Barry Grove, Managing Director) in New York City. Its cast was as follows:

CUSTOMER ....John Rubinstein
DMV LADY ....E. Katherine Kerr

AUTHOR'S NOTE

This is a simple sketch about a man trying to renew his license at the Division of Motor Vehicles.

I think we all live in fear of places like the Division of Motor Vehicles, which I why I wrote the piece.

CHARACTERS

CUSTOMER
DMV LADY

DMV TYRANT

Scene: A window at the Division of Motor Vehicles. Sign on desk reads "Division of Motor Vehicles."

A Woman at a window (DMV Lady), approached by a Customer.

CUSTOMER. Is this Window 7?

DMV LADY. Yes?

CUSTOMER. I'm afraid something rather complicated has happened with my driver's license.

DMV LADY. I'm sorry to hear that. What happened? *(With great disinterest she begins to read a book.)*

CUSTOMER. Well, you see, I moved here from another state, and I let my driver's license lapse ... and.... *(Waits.)*

DMV LADY. *(Looks up.)* Yes?

CUSTOMER. Should I wait until you finish?

DMV LADY. I don't think so. It's a very long book.

CUSTOMER. But ... are you listening to my problem?

DMV LADY. I can read and listen at the same time. Go on. *(Goes back to reading.)*

CUSTOMER. Oh. Well. Uh, anyway, I took the driving test again, and I passed it and got this temporary license, which has now expired, and I've never gotten my permanent one, and when I called about it, they said they had lost me in the computer, and they had no record of my taking the test, and so they couldn't send me my license even though I did take and pass the test. *(Pause.)* Your turn to say something.

DMV LADY. Wait a minute. *(Reads some more. Looks up.)* I wanted to finish the paragraph. Now what seems to be the matter?

CUSTOMER. Well....

DMV LADY. In one sentence.

CUSTOMER. I haven't received my drivers license.

DMV LADY. Let me see if you're on the computer.

CUSTOMER. I'm not on the computer.

DMV LADY. What is your name?

CUSTOMER. I'm not there.

DMV LADY. How do you spell that?

CUSTOMER. I'm not on the computer. I went to Window 3, and they told me there was no record of me on the computer.

DMV LADY. I am not Window 3, I am Window 7, and I need to know your name.

CUSTOMER. James Agnes.

DMV LADY. Is that a as in aardvark, g as in *gesundheit*, n as in nincompoop, e as in excruciating, s as in seltzer water, pause pause, j as in Jupiter, a as in Agnes, m as in Mary, e as in excruciating, and s as in slow, lingering death?

CUSTOMER. Yes.

DMV LADY. *(Types into computer; looks.)* Well, you're not on the computer.

CUSTOMER. I told you I wasn't.

DMV LADY. Fine. I will give you an award at the end of the day. How else may I help you?

CUSTOMER. I ... I would like to get my permanent license.

DMV LADY. I'm sorry. There is no record of you on the computer.

CUSTOMER. Yes, but I have my temporary license. *(Hands it to her.)*

DMV LADY. This temporary license has expired.

CUSTOMER. Yes, I know it's expired.

DMV LADY. It is no longer a valid license.

CUSTOMER. I know that. That's why I want my permanent one. I hadn't noticed it hadn't come in the mail until this one had already expired. I had presumed everything was all right.

DMV LADY. What a funny thing to do. *(Suspicious.)* If you do not have a valid driver's license, how did you get here to the Division of Motor Vehicles?

CUSTOMER. I took a taxi.

DMV LADY. Can you prove that to me?

CUSTOMER. What?

DMV LADY. Did you keep a receipt from the taxi?

CUSTOMER. No, I didn't.

DMV LADY. I trust you did not drive here yourself, did you, Mr. James Agnes?

CUSTOMER. No, no, I realize my license is not valid.

DMV LADY. That is correct. You have an invalid license. Good morning.

CUSTOMER. But you're not helping me.

DMV LADY. *(Pleasantly.)* How may I help you?

CUSTOMER. I want my driver's license.

DMV LADY. You must take the driving test.

CUSTOMER. But I took the driving test.

DMV LADY. I have no record of that.

CUSTOMER. I know you have no record of it, some *schmuck* lost it in the computer …

DMV LADY. Kindly do not speak Yiddish to me. If you wish to make an appointment to take the driving test, go to Window 4. *(Goes back to reading.)*

CUSTOMER. I DON'T WANT TO TAKE THE TEST AGAIN!

DMV LADY. *(Irritated.)* Well, when did you take the test before?

CUSTOMER. It's the same date as that on my temporary license.

DMV LADY. February 3, 1888. The Division of Motor Vehicles did not exist in 1888.

CUSTOMER. Let me see that. *(Looks.)* All right, it's a typo. It's clearly meant to be *1988*.

DMV LADY. I am willing to agree with you that it is most likely a typo. You see, I don't stick to the rules on everything, I am human. What is your name again?

CUSTOMER. Agnes, James.

DMV LADY. Is that a as in aardvark, g as in *gesundheit* …

CUSTOMER. Agnes, James!

DMV LADY. Let me see if we have a record of you in the computer. *(Types into computer.)*

CUSTOMER. You don't, you don't, I told you you don't!

DMV LADY. Why are you shouting at me? When I am shouted at, I do not feel like cooperating.

CUSTOMER. But you haven't *been* cooperating.

DMV LADY. I have been cooperating. If I had not been

cooperating, you would have been shouting at me much earlier than this.

CUSTOMER. I want my license.

DMV LADY. Well, you can't have it. You're not on the computer.

CUSTOMER. But that's not my fault.

DMV LADY. And it's not my fault. We are both blameless. Isn't it a nice feeling?

CUSTOMER. You are not helping me.

DMV LADY. I am doing everything in my power.

CUSTOMER. But don't you have more power than you're using? Can't you, for instance, type me into the computer, and then send me my license?

DMV LADY. No. Only the secretary at the driving test site can do that.

CUSTOMER. But when she forgets to do that at the time of the driving test, can't someone else do it then?

DMV LADY. If the secretary at the driving test site is willing to write a note admitting that she has forgotten to type in your name, then I can enter your name into the computer. And then we will fire here. Do you want her to lose her job?

CUSTOMER. No, I don't. I want you to lose *your* job.

DMV LADY. I don't see how you can expect me to help you if you're going to be hostile.

CUSTOMER. Isn't there anything you can suggest to solve my problem?

DMV LADY. *(Thinks.)* If you could relive the initial driving test, when it was finished, you could ask to watch the secretary type in your name and your test result into the computer.

CUSTOMER. Your suggestion is that I *relive* the initial driving test?

DMV LADY. It is a hypothetical suggestion, I admit, but it is the limit of what I can think of to assist you.

CUSTOMER. Could I see your supervisor please?

DMV LADY. My supervisor is shredding documents in the other room, and cannot be disturbed.

CUSTOMER. *(Angry.)* Look into my eyes. I want you to tell me what I should do that will solve my problem, and I want you to tell me *right now!*

DMV LADY.   Move out of New York.

CUSTOMER.   *(Taken aback, but it might be worth it.)* That's a good suggestion. Thank you. *(He storms out.)*

DMV LADY.   *(Calling after him.)* Ohio's nice. *(She goes back to reading.)*

END

PROPERTY LIST

Book (DMV LADY)
Temporary license (CUSTOMER)

GYM TEACHER

GYM TEACHER was first presented as part of A MESS OF PLAYS BY CHRIS DURANG at South Coast Repertory (David Emmes, Producing Artistic Director; Martin Benson, Artistic Director) in Costa Mesa, California, in spring, 1996. It was directed by David Chambers; the set design was by Michael C. Smith; the costume design was by Todd Roehrman; the lighting design was by Tom Ruzika; the sound and video design were by Garth Hemphill; the production manager was Michael Mora; and the stage manager was Randall K. Lum. It was performed by Howard Shangraw as MR. ORLANDO.

Subsequently, this sketch was part of MIX AND MATCH DURANG at the John Drew Theatre in East Hampton, New York, in June 1997, with Peter Jacobson as MR. ORLANDO.

GYM TEACHER

Lights up on Mr. Orlando, in a shirt and tie, slacks. On the floor next to him is a gym bag. He is somewhat macho, kind of like an ex-Marine. He barks orders a lot, tells people how things are going to be.

MR. ORLANDO.   Good morning, boys and girls. I'm Mr. Orlando. I'm going to be your teacher in *physical* education and in *health* education. You got it? And there's a lot more to health than just taking Nyquil when you've got a cold, I can tell ya that. *(Smiles.)* Bet you never expected to get anyone like me for a teacher, did you? *(Takes off tie.)*

I'm not a teacher, I'm just a regular guy. My first name is Bucky.

So, it's phys ed, health; and sometimes literature. Anybody ever read Erica Jong? Well, she's a cool chick, we're gonna read her while doing jumping jacks sometimes.

But first we're gonna play a really fun game called Bombardment where everybody throws medicine balls at one another until everybody gets hit and nobody's left standing. Anyone know what a medicine ball is? Well, it's like a volley ball, only it's heavier. It's good for you.

Okay, boys line up on one side, girls on the other side. Hurry up, little girl, no pussyfooting in my class. Move your ass. *(Grins, friendly to the boys.)*

Get that, guys? No *pussy*footing? *(Back to business; lifts up his arm.)*

See all this sweat? That's sweat, God damn it. You're all going to be sweating a lot now, your glands are gonna be poppin' like hell. That happens in the seventh grade. *(Grins at some 13-year-old boy.)* Right, shorty? *(Laughs.)*

Hi there, little girl. That's quite a pair of knockers you got there. Hey, don't look offended, I'm just kiddin'. Come on! I want us to have fun in this class. *(Announcement to class at large:)*

Anybody who doesn't have a sense of humor, I want them to get one before the end of class. Is that clear? Good. *(Laughs, takes off his shirt; is bare-chested.)*

I never wear an undershirt. Never saw any reason to. Hell, I'm not cold. *(Slaps his chest.)*

Now some people think that girls and guys should take gym class separately. Well, we don't have money to have two teachers, so you're gonna take it together, and you're gonna like it. *(To boy.)*

Hey, shorty! What you got your hands in your pocket for? Get 'em outta there. Don't act innocent with me, I wasn't born yesterday.

Anybody gets a boner gets thrown in the shower and then hung upside down over the toilet while we flush the john. Is that clear?

Whaddya looking confused about, little girl? You don't know what a boner is? Ask your mother. Ask your father. Write a letter to the mayor, he'll tell you.

Okay, listen up. Seventh grade is a tough time of life. You're leaving childhood behind, and you're entering the world of glands and nocturnal emissions and women's "time of the month" — you guys don't know what that is? Believe me, you don't want to know. And condoms and jock straps and bras and panties and orgies with twenty people.

So it's a stressful time. And so we gotta get some of the stress out in gym class. And so we run around like crazy throwing balls and climbing ropes and jumping up and down on the trampoline and sweating and straining and just knocking ourselves out.

And team spirit. Don't forget about team spirit. Later today we're going to have a pep rally, and you're gonna scream your fuckin' lungs out.

You with me so far? *(Smells under his arm.)*

I don't believe in deodorant. That's for fairies. Nothing wrong with natural sweat smell. Anybody in this class a fairy? Anybody in this class is a fairy we're gonna throw him in the shower with all his clothes off and then hang him upside down over the toilet while someone flushes the john. We'll be doing a lot of that in gym class this year.

Okay. Listen up. Now we're gonna play Bombardment, or sometimes it's called War, or sometimes it's called make the medicine ball smack against the sensitive skin of Irish people so their white skin turns bright pink and smarts all day. *(Looks around.)*

Any blue-eyed, light-skinned Irish people here today? Nice red hair, buddy. You're gonna have big pink welts all over you in a couple minutes unless you're cagey duckin' that ball. You know how to duck the ball? Well that's the object of this game. Duck the ball, or you get hit and you're out.

Okay. Listen up. Now to play Bombardment, we need a couple of balls. *(Leers.)*

Any volunteers, guys? *(Laughs.)* Okay, sissies. We'll use the balls I brought. *(Takes two heavy bowling balls out of his gym bag.)*

Now the school didn't have money to buy any medicine balls, so I brung these bowling balls from home. Anybody who doesn't like them is a fairy. We got any fairies? I didn't think so. You guys can get muscles tossing these guys around. Good for you.

Okay, ready? The guys'll be shirts and the girls'll be skins. Come on, ladies. Get those blouses off. *(Catches a look from the little who girl who objected to the "knockers" discussion earlier.)*

Look, little girl, don't you make faces at me. What did I tell you about getting a sense of humor? I want you to get one, and I wanna see it fast! You got me?

Okay … that's right. Shirts, skins. Don't feel bad if your breasts are small. Some guys have small dicks too, it evens out. That's one of the things we're gonna learn in health class. But for now, we're just gonna have some *fun. (Lifts up the bowling balls with a maniacal glint in his eyes.)*

Everybody ready?? Here come the balls!!!! *(He goes to throw them. Lights black. The sound of bowling balls crashing into people and onto the ground. Terrible thuds and screams.)*

PROPERTY LIST

Gym bag with 2 bowling balls

1-900-DESPERATE

CHARACTERS

GRETCHEN, home alone
RECORDED VOICE (male)
SALLY, over-anxious
ZELDA, mysterious
LITTLE BOY, age 5 or so
SCUZZY, sexy, stupid 20-year-old guy

NOTE: The little boy is written to be played by a real little boy; though I suppose it could also be done by a young man (or even young woman). If it was done sincerely enough, the audience would probably accept the convention that an older actor was standing in for a child in the sketch. But it should not seem that the older person was "pretending" to be a child on the phone line; that's the danger of not using a child to play the little boy.

1-900-DESPERATE

Scene: Gretchen, a woman in her mid-30s, is on the phone.

Elsewhere on the stage are other people seated in chairs, who eventually will be on the phone also.

But for now, lights only on Gretchen.

GRETCHEN.   No, mother, I don't have a date tonight. I know it's Saturday night. Yes I know my sister Rebecca is married and has children. I've met the children. Yes, they're lovely ... *(Listens.)*

Well, I'm sorry my life makes you unhappy, mother. I'm very happy here alone in my apartment on Saturday. Oh I don't know. Maybe I'll rent a video tonight. Or eat an entire cake. No, I'm kidding. You know I don't keep food in the house. I have water and baking soda, so if I get acid indigestion from not eating anything, I'm well prepared. *(Listens some more; holds her head.)*

Mother, please don't say that about me, you make me feel worthless and desperate. No, I don't want you to lie to me. No, I take that back — I *do* want you to lie to me. Tell me it's fine that I'm alone on Saturday night, and I'm fine. Say that, mother. *Say it. (Listens; it's brief.)*

Uh huh. That's very good. Now the other part. Uh huh. Good. Thank you, mother, it's very sweet of you to feel that way. Now I have to go put my frozen dinner in the microwave, so let me hang up.... I don't feel like cooking, mother.... Well, I get radiation at the dentist too.... Let's drop it, let me get off the phone now. Good night. *(Grouchy.)*

Yes, I love you too. *(Hangs up.)*

Oh, thank God, I'm off the phone. *(Looks around; disoriented.)*

But what should I do now? Oh, I feel desperate.

VOICE.   Feeling desperate? Then call 1-900-DESPERATE. That special someone may just be waiting for you.

GRETCHEN.   Oh, Lord, now I'm hearing voices. Oh that's right, the TV is on. I guess that was on the TV. Oh good, I'm not crazy. I'm not crazy. I'm just desperate. *(Starts to dial.)* 1-900-Desperate. *(As soon as Gretchen finishes dialing, we hear the sound of ringing. Then a click, and a recorded voice.)*

RECORDED VOICE.   Hello there, swinging singles. You have reached 1-900-Desperate, where you can meet the man or woman of your dreams. The call costs $1.99 a half minute, $3.98 for a full minute. And there is a $25 minimum for six minutes and 28 seconds. If you don't want to be charged, hang up now. Too late. *(Gretchen is taken aback. She might have hung up, but it happened too fast.)* You didn't hang up immediately, you might as well listen in on the line, we're going to charge you whatever you do. Enjoy yourself! *(There is another click, and lights come up on the some of the other people who are talking or listening on this 1-900 party line. We see Sally, who is extremely over-anxious to make a connection with someone. She is either not too attractive, or doesn't think she is. Maybe has a bottle of something, but she is not drunk. Her desperation keeps her sober. And we also see Zelda, who looks highly intelligent and sardonic. She seems to be on the line for purposes other than of meeting people.)*

SALLY.   *(Having heard the click of Gretchen coming on the line.)* Hello?

GRETCHEN.   *(Tentative.)* Hello?

SALLY.   Are there any men on this line?

GRETCHEN.   Is this 1-900-Desperate?

SALLY.   It sure is. Are you a man with a high voice?

GRETCHEN.   No, I'm a woman.

SALLY.   Damn it. Any men out there?

ZELDA.   We've got to stop looking to men to give us meaning.

SALLY.   Who the fuck is that?

GRETCHEN.   I think she's right. I have meaning even though I'm home alone on Saturday, thinking of renting a video and using the microwave.

ZELDA. You mean to kill yourself.

GRETCHEN. No. To cook.

SALLY. Hello? Any men there? *(Lights up on a little boy.)*

LITTLE BOY. Hello?

SALLY. Are you a man?

LITTLE BOY. I'm five years old.

SALLY. Oh, great.

LITTLE BOY. My name is Billy.

SALLY. I don't care what your name is, shut up.

GRETCHEN. Please, don't be abusive to a child.

SALLY. Oh, God, why are there no men on the line?

LITTLE BOY. *(Calls.)* I'm not doing anything, mommy. *(To the phone.)* Bye! *(Little Boy hangs up, lights go off him.)*

GRETCHEN. I guess I'd hang up too, but ...

SALLY. But what?

GRETCHEN. Well, I guess I've paid for it.

SALLY. Uh huh. Any men out there? Please God.

ZELDA. Women were once warriers. We hunted like Diana, we carved the turkeys at dinner. We must return to those times.

SALLY. Will you shut up?

ZELDA. You need a women's support group.

SALLY. I need a man. I don't need women yapping at me. *(Lights come up on Scuzzy, a kind of sexy 20-year-old with slicked-back hair and a leather jacket.)*

SCUZZY. Hey, ladies, how's it hangin'?

SALLY. Oh my God, a man! Hello! Hello!

SCUZZY. You ladies feelin' desperate tonight?

ZELDA. Not really. I'm reading the diaries of Anais Nin. She was very spiritual.

SCUZZY. Hey, ladies, I'm 18. How old are you?

SALLY. I'm 20. *(She's much older.)*

ZELDA. I'm 105.

SCUZZY. Anyone else out there?

GRETCHEN. Yes. Although I can't stay long. I dialed by mistake.

SCUZZY. Ooooo. A happy mistake for me. What's your name, baby?

GRETCHEN. My name is ... Gretchen.

SALLY.   My name is Sally.

SCUZZY.   What you look like, Gretchen?

GRETCHEN.   Oh ... I don't know.

SALLY.   I look like a model. I have large breats and a tiny waist and ... do you like big or small hips?

SCUZZY.   Who is this? I'm talkin' to Gretchen.

SALLY.   Well, I can't lie. I have small hips. And blond hair and bright red lips and I've studied the Kama-Sutra.

SCUZZY.   Hey, Gretchen, talk to Scuzzy again.

GRETCHEN.   Hello.

SCUZZY.   Hey, baby, you sound hot.

GRETCHEN.   What kind of name is Scuzzy?

SCUZZY.   It's my nickname. You got a nickname?

GRETCHEN.   Gretchen. Well, it's not a nickname ... it's a name.

SCUZZY.   So, what you want, baby?

GRETCHEN.   Oh, I don't know.

SALLY.   Sometimes I have an orgasm just walking down the street. That's the kind of passionate person I am.

SCUZZY.   Butt out, butt head. I'm talkin' to Gretchen. Gretchen, you still there?

GRETCHEN.   Yes. Hello. How are you? Where's the woman reading Anais Nin?

ZELDA.   Women don't need men.

SCUZZY.   Oh yeah? How ya gonna fertilize your eggs then?

GRETCHEN.   Excuse me. I think I'm going to get off now.

SCUZZY.   You want me to call you?

GRETCHEN.   Call me??

SCUZZY.   You know. On your number. We can have a "better talk" that way.

GRETCHEN.   Oh, I don't know, I don't feel I know you properly yet.

SCUZZY.   What do you want to know?

GRETCHEN.   Oh, gosh. What books do you read?

SCUZZY.   Books. I read the *TV Guide.*

GRETCHEN.   Yes, that's a good publication. *(Lights back up on the Little Boy.)*

LITTLE BOY.   I have a little red wagon.

SCUZZY. Who the hell is that?

SALLY. Oh, I give up. I hate you all! *(Sally hangs up. Lights go down on her.)*

SCUZZY. Gretchen, I wanna call you, baby. Give me your number.

GRETCHEN. Well, I don't know.

SCUZZY. What do you look like, Gretchen?

GRETCHEN. Oh, I don't know.

SCUZZY. You don't know?

GRETCHEN. Well, let's see. I'm 5'9", I have brown eyes.

SCUZZY. What are your measurements? Heh, heh, heh.

GRETCHEN. Um ...my measurements are 36-46-77. I look like a large teepee. And I invite men up to my lair and poison them at dinner and serve their bodies to the racoons outside my house.

SCUZZY. Oooooh, this lady's intriguing!

ZELDA. Good for you, Gretchen. Feed him to the racoons.

SCUZZY. We got a nut case on the line. Shut up, nut case! Hey, Gretchen, baby, gimme your number.

GRETCHEN. I'm sorry. I don't think we're right for one another. I'm sorry, Scuzzy. I'm sure you're very nice, for someone.

SCUZZY. Damn right I am. *(There is a pause.)*

LITTLE BOY. I have a little doggie, and a big doggie.

SCUZZY. Any hot chicks on the line?

ZELDA. *(With a glint, does a feminine, girlish voice.)* I'm here. Who's this?

SCUZZY. My name is Scuzzy.

ZELDA. Oh, I think I'm gonna like you, Scuzzy. Can I give you a good time?

SCUZZY. What's your number?

ZELDA. Let me call you.

SCUZZY. Okay. My number's 666-0666.

ZELDA. Ooooh, that's a sexy number.

SCUZZY. I'm a sexy guy.

ZELDA. I'll call you right up.

SCUZZY. Okay, baby. *(Scuzzy hangs up. Lights go off of him.)*

ZELDA. *(Regular voice.)* Good night, Gretchen. I'm gonna

97

make him suffer. And all for you, baby. And for women everywhere. *(Zelda hangs up. Lights off of her. Now only Gretchen and the
Little Boy are lit.)*

GRETCHEN. Well, calling this line has been a terrific success.

LITTLE BOY. I have a little red wagon.

GRETCHEN. Do you? That's nice.

LITTLE BOY. My mommy and daddy are asleep in front of
the television.

GRETCHEN. I wish I could sleep.

LITTLE BOY. I'm five.

GRETCHEN. I'm 35. I guess I could consider waiting for you.
In 15 years, you'll be 20.

LITTLE BOY. I have a boo boo on my knee.

GRETCHEN. I don't think this relationship is going to work
out.

LITTLE BOY. I can tie my shoelaces.

GRETCHEN. On the other hand, that's better than a lot of
the men I know, I'm starting to get interested again.

LITTLE BOY. I have two doggies.

GRETCHEN. Uh huh.

LITTLE BOY. And one's small, and one's big.

GRETCHEN. Really?

LITTLE BOY. And I have a teddy bear named Fred.

GRETCHEN. Uh huh …

LITTLE BOY. And I can count to ten, and some higher numbers too.

GRETCHEN. Uh huh.

LITTLE BOY. One, two …

GRETCHEN. Uh huh.

LITTLE BOY. Three, four, five.

GRETCHEN. Really. How interesting.

LITTLE BOY. Five. And six. And seven.

GRETCHEN. Uh huh.… *(Lights dim on the Little Boy counting
and Gretchen going "uh huh."…)*

ONE MINUTE PLAY

ONE MINUTE PLAY was written for a benefit for the American Repertory Theatre in Cambridge, Massachusetts, some time in the spring of 1992. The cast of this brief play was as follows:

POLLY..Anne Pitoniak
DAVE..Michael Malone Starr

AUTHOR'S NOTE

I wrote this for a "one minute play festival" to benefit the American Repertory Theatre in Camridge, Massassachutts.

The previous time I wrote them a "one minute" play it was actually seven minutes (ENTERTAINING MR. HELMS, later in this volume). So this time I wanted to really have it be only one minute.

CHARACTERS

POLLY
DAVE

SETTING

Somewhere. Dave and Polly are sitting or standing. They've just run into one another. Polly is light-spirited, airy, in a good mood.

ONE MINUTE PLAY

POLLY.   Hello, Dave, how are you?

DAVE.   Well, I don't have a sense of myself today. I feel rather worthless. Do you think of me as worthless?

POLLY.   Oh, I don't know. I was just trying to make a pleasantry.

DAVE.   You know my wife left me. She married my father. He's 80, but she prefers him.

POLLY.   Gee, I'm sorry to hear that. Are there any restaurants you can recommend? My Aunt Helen is coming to town.

DAVE.   I'm thinking of going out to find a copy of *Final Exit.* Is that the correct title? Do you have a copy?

POLLY.   Gosh, no, I never read books. I don't have the time.

DAVE.   I have a lot of time now that I've been fired.

POLLY.   Gee, I didn't know you'd been fired. What happened?

DAVE.   Well, I was incompetent. I don't know why they hired me.

POLLY.   What was your profession exactly?

DAVE.   Well, it's hard to say really.

POLLY.   Well, forget it then, I don't want to know. And you can't recommend a restaurant, I guess?

DAVE.   I've lost my appetite. I'm not sleeping. I'm losing weight, and my hair is falling out.

POLLY.   *(Stares at him.)* Well, you know, I hope this isn't some call for psychological help that I'm not picking up, but basically I think you're just having a really bad day, and I'm sure you'll feel a lot better tomorrow. And you know, your wife — well, she was rubbish, good riddance. Your father, so he's sexy for an 80 year old. Your job, you didn't like it anyway. And you needed to lose some weight, so all this sleep loss and body loss is really quite attractive. So tomorrow you'll see it all differently. Well, good-bye. *(Exits.)*

DAVE.   *(Calling after her.)* Tomorrow I'll see things differently. Tomorrow I'll be dead. Oh you there! I haven't finished talking to you. *(Pause.)* I've thought of a good restaurant! *(Pause.)* But you'll never get the name of it from me. So long. Good riddance. *(Pause; to himself with some comfort.)* Well, death tomorrow.

WOMEN IN A PLAYGROUND

AUTHOR'S NOTE

I wrote WOMEN IN A PLAYGROUND and the piece that follows it, PHYLLIS AND XENOBIA, a long time ago, in 1975.

At that time I got a part-time position teaching acting twice a week at Southern Connecticut Teachers College. I felt not too terribly qualified to do this job. Though I had just received a Masters from Yale School of Drama, it was in playwriting, not acting; except for one singing class with the Yale actors, I had never actually taken any acting classes. But they needed a replacement teacher, and I needed the job.

I figured out most of what to do by reading Viola Spolin's book on theatre games. And as the semester went on, I started to get more confidence, and I began to bring in short scenes I wrote specifically for the class to experiment with acting intention and so on.

WOMEN IN A PLAYGROUND and the odder PHYLLIS AND XENOBIA are the only two I can still find.

And reading WOMEN IN A PLAYGROUND now, I see that it was an early draft in my head of the playground scene that later showed up again, considerably darker, in BABY WITH THE BATHWATER.

Well, so that's where these two playlets come from.

CHARACTERS

ETHEL, fairly happy
ALICE, not too happy

WOMEN IN A PLAYGROUND

Ethel and Alice, sitting on a bench. Sounds of a playground. They look out to see their children.

ETHEL. Which one is yours?

ALICE. What? Oh, the little boy in the blue jacket.

ETHEL. Oh. That's a nice jacket.

ALICE. Yes. *(Silence.)* Which one is yours?

ETHEL. That's Mary playing with your son.

ALICE. Oh, yes.

ETHEL. She's five.

ALICE. Oh. She's a pretty child.

ETHEL. She's very well behaved and never gives me a moment of worry.

ALICE. That must be nice for you. *(Silence.)*

ETHEL. How old is your son?

ALICE. He's five also.

ETHEL. What's his name?

ALICE. James.

ETHEL. James. Do you call him Jimmy?

ALICE. No. Not yet.

ETHEL. But you might?

ALICE. No, I don't think we will. James. *(Silence.)*

ETHEL. Does he give you any trouble?

ALICE. Not yet. *(Looks at him with grim foreboding.)*

ETHEL. That's nice he hasn't given you any trouble.

ALICE. Well, you never know when he'll start though.

ETHEL. That's sort of a pessimistic attitude to take.

ALICE. Oh, I am pessimistic.

ETHEL. I'm an optimist, and me and my husband are very happy.

ALICE. Are you?

ETHEL. Yes, we are.

ALICE. Well, that may change.

ETHEL.   I hope not.

ALICE.   We all hope not, but that doesn't stop things changing.

ETHEL.   I don't think I could stand to have your attitude. I wouldn't want to get up in the mornings.

ALICE.   And you do now?

ETHEL.   Of course I do.

ALICE.   Why?

ETHEL.   Well, to make breakfast for my husband. Bill. And for my little girl Mary. And to take Mary to the playground. And to see what the day has in store.

ALICE.   To see what's in store, eh?

ETHEL.   Yes.

ALICE.   I don't see why anyone would be anxious for that. Lots of terrible things can be in store.

ETHEL.   Well, of course, I know that. I may be an optimist, but I'm no Pollyanna. But you have to proceed as *if* things will be all right, you have to proceed that way, or you'll never get things done.

ALICE.   You've gotten that philosophy from some saying or other. You sound like the back of a match pack.

ETHEL.   Well, I hope you don't give your philosophy to your little boy. You'll have a suicide case on your hands before he's eight.

ALICE.   Six. Look, they're climbing up the slide. Do you think either one will fall off? *(Ethel looks at Alice with dislike and worry. Alice keeps looking out. Lights fade.)*

PHYLLIS AND XENOBIA

CHARACTERS

PHYLLIS, controlling and rather cheerful.
XENOBIA, her sister, unhappy and rather resistant.

PHYLLIS AND XENOBIA

*Scene: The kitchen of Phyllis and Xenobia. Pretty, feminine, fussy
curtains and kitchen table cloth, etc. etc. Phyllis and Xenobia are
sisters. They can be as young as 35, or as old as 65. Both wear
print dresses with busy tiny flower patterns on them.*

*They're sitting at the kitchen table, chatting and maybe having
tea, like they do every day of their lives.*

PHYLLIS.   I like pudding. I like vanilla pudding and choco-
late pudding and tapioca pudding and butterscotch pudding.
XENOBIA.   I don't like pudding.
PHYLLIS.   I do. I like pudding.
XENOBIA.   I know. I don't though.
PHYLLIS.   Yes you do. Oh, the puddings our mother used to
make. And the cookies. She used to bake dozens and dozens
of cookies a day. And you know where she put 'em?
XENOBIA.   I don't like cookies. I never have. I never will.
They're not good for you.
PHYLLIS.   Well, what is, these days? *(Fondly remembering.)* She
used to put them all over the room. In the cookie jars, of
course. But under the sofa, and behind the sofa pillows, and
behind the china cabinet, under the carpets, behind the curtains, embedded in the floor boards, in little holes in the walls,
up above the door frames — just everywhere you looked, there
were cookies. That woman was obsessed with cookies.
XENOBIA.   She was a bad housekeeper, mother was. She
never should have done that. We got bugs everywhere.
PHYLLIS.   You're right, we did. It started, of course, with the
rugs, that's where the bugs started. But they didn't stop there.
I didn't mind them though. Did you?
XENOBIA.   Yes, I did mind the bugs. I couldn't stand them.
PHYLLIS.   Well, you learn to stand everything after awhile,
don't you? *(Suddenly reaches over and hits Xenobia hard on the side*

113

of her head. Xenobia is shocked and angry.)

XENOBIA. What did you do that for?

PHYLLIS. You had a bug in your hair.

XENOBIA. I didn't!

PHYLLIS. You did.

XENOBIA. I did *not* have a bug there. I did *not.*

PHYLLIS. Either you had a bug in your hair, or you're wearing a bobby pin that crawls on little legs. And for your sake I hope it's bugs. *(Hits her in the head again.)* There's another one! *(Xenobia looks shocked and upset. Stares at Phyllis. They're silent for a moment.)*

XENOBIA. I hated mother. I'm glad I killed her.

PHYLLIS. Xenobia, you've got to stop thinking you did it. Stephen did it. We saw him do it, and then we watched him be put away, don't you remember?

XENOBIA. I'd like a cookie now.

PHYLLIS. You can't have one. You don't want one. *(Xenobia thinks for a second.)*

XENOBIA. I killed mother. I remember. Because she was in the kitchen and she was making French toast and she was dipping the bread into the egg batter, and she was spreading little chocolate nuggets on the floor with her feet for the baby to eat, and I remember thinking, THIS WOMAN IS CRAZY! So I picked up a mop ...

PHYLLIS. No, no, no, no, it wasn't that way at all. It was much more pleasant for one thing. And it was egg merringues, not French toast. Light and fluffy and filled with egg-y goodness. It was like eating an angel's head.

XENOBIA. Well, it doesn't really matter whether it was egg merringues or French toast, the point is that mother's dead, and now we can keep the house clean again. Only you won't let us. You're always hiding Tasty Cakes underneath the sofa, and behind the curtains, and in the cabinets. You're no better than mother. You're just like mother. My doctor says I shouldn't live with you anymore. He says I should ... *(Pause.)*

PHYLLIS. Should? Should what?

XENOBIA. *(Thinks; evasive.)* Should not live with you anymore. *(Pause.)*

114

PHYLLIS. You do like pudding.
XENOBIA. I don't.
PHYLLIS. You do.
XENOBIA. I don't.
PHYLLIS. You do.
XENOBIA. I don't. *(Phyllis hits Xenobia in the arm.)*
PHYLLIS. Another bug.

JOHN AND MARY DOE

JOHN AND MARY DOE was first performed as part of A MESS OF PLAYS BY CHRIS DURANG at South Coast Repertory, in Costa Mesa, California, in 1996. Directed by David Chambers, the play was the opening play of the evening, and the cast was as follows:

JOHN DOE..Hal Landon, Jr.
MARY DOE ....Amanda Carlin
JOHN, JR. ....Howard Shangraw
JOHN THE SECOND ....Robert Patrick Benedict
JOHNNA ....Jodi Thelen

AUTHOR'S NOTE

Listening to angry anti-government (and especially anti-liberal) radio commentators, it seems to me that many in the country seem riveted by a desire to live back in the 1950s, when life seemed simpler (at least in retrospect). And though I think it's foolish to try to return to the past — it's not a do-able thing, and there are lots of stupid things about the 1950s that we're forgetting in our haze — still it's equally foolish to pretend that our present times aren't upsetting. These two conflicting thoughts are the themes fueling this short play.

CHARACTERS

JOHN DOE, an upstanding husband in his late 30s
MARY DOE, an upstanding wife in her 30s
JOHN, JR., their son
JOHN THE SECOND, their other son
JOHNNA, their daughter

JOHN AND MARY DOE

JOHN. Hello. My name is John Doe. That is my name, I do not mean that I am a representative everyman. That is my family-given name. My middle name is Ferdinand, if it helps you distinguish me. My name is John Ferdinand Doe. John Doe for short.

My wife's name is Mary Doe. Her maiden name was Smith. We met in elementary school. She was always very sweet, and I knew I wanted to marry her the moment I met her when we were nine. I never went through that period of hating girls. No, I was firmly heterosexual even at age nine.

My wife's middle name, to help distinguish her in your mind, is Mother of God. Her name is Mary Mother of God Doe, nee Mary Mother of God Smith.

We have three children. John Jr., John the Second, and our daughter Johnna, Daughter of Mother of God Doe.

We have three pets. We have a dog named Sputnik. And we have a cat named John F. Kennedy, Jr. And we have a gold fish we call Jason Robards, Jr. My son sometimes dresses up in drag and pretends to be Lauren Bacall.

My wife and I have never molested our children. Or if we have, we've forgotten it entirely. And we hope they have. We are not attracted to children anyway. We are attracted to one another, and sometimes to other couples, and sometimes we have drunken orgies, but I don't think we've really done that, I'm just kidding. Absence makes the heart grow fonder.

Why did I say that I wonder. Oh yes. My wife Mary Mother of God Doe nee Smith was murdered last year by our next door neighbor, Tommy Psycho Babbit. We miss my wife very much, Tommy and I do. Tommy is in a mental institution. We all agree he's crazy. We all forgive him for killing my wife, and we all hope he gets better and that he's learning skills that he can use in the outside world, skills like getting mail from the mail box without axing someone to death and hiding parts of their bodies around the yard like some sort of demented Easter egg hunt. Do you remember Easter egg hunts? Weren't they fun? How I miss my childhood, all the good times. I wish I could be four years old again.

We still haven't found my wife's knees. I sometimes get afraid opening certain drawers in the house, afraid we'll find them. Tommy Psycho Babbit swears he never put any of her body parts in the house, but then we did find that Adam's apple in the refrigerator. Of course, my wife didn't have an Adam's apple, so it didn't belong to her. We don't know who it belonged to.

I'm sorry. Is this becoming gruesome? Do you wish this were going to be nicer? Let me start over.

Everything I've said has been a lie. Nothing bad has happened in our family, I just told you all this awful stuff because I wanted to get you to like me. And also to upset you. And also to give you nightmares. But I know where to draw the line. I think the line should be drawn right now. No more awful things from me. Only nice things.

My daughter Johnna drew a picture of a snowman today. My wife Mary and I put it up on the refrigerator. And then we gave Johnna a warm, parental, non-sexual hug, and we told her we love her. Then my wife played Chopin on the piano, with Johnna tied to the piano leg and filled up with enema water, which she was not allowed to expel. *Sybil* was one of my wife's favorite movies, and try and try as we do, her therapist and I cannot get her to stop torturing little Johnna with enemas.

Who invented the enema? Was it a caveman who had indigestion? He had just invented the wheel, and so then he invented the hose, and water pressure, and he thought! I know! I think I'll stick this hose up my ass, that should be fun.

Let me start over. I've gotten disturbing again.

Lovely little duckies frolicking in the water. Beautiful delicate butterflies landing on pretty yellow flowers and daintily sipping nectar. Fuzzy big bumble bees who make a nice sound but don't want to sting people floating about in the summer sun. Endangered species frolicking in a waterfall and being force-fed Prozac by Dr. Kevorkian.

I think if you want to die you should every goddamn right to do it. I think if you want to have Dr. Kevorkian or some other doctor you know come over and give you a delicious cocktail that'll kill you, or hook you up some sort of gas-inhaler or something ... well, I say, bully for you, and so long!

And now the first scene. *(John and his wife Mary.)* Mary. I love you.

MARY. And John. I love you.

JOHN. Mary, I love you.

MARY. And I love you, John.

JOHN. Mary, I love you.

MARY. Yes, thank you. I cherish your love, John.

JOHN. And I cherish your love, Mary. And now the second scene.

MARY. John, I'm concerned about our country.

JOHN. You are? What about it?

MARY. Well, I feel there is a lack of morality now. The children seem to carry guns in school now. We never did that when I was younger. Why are they carrying guns?

JOHN. Let's ask them. John Jr., John the Second. Why are you carrying guns to school now?

JOHN JR. It's cool. Also, we have to protect ourselves from Tommy Psycho Babbit who lives next door.

MARY. Oh, that's right. I think I'm dead. I think I'm dismembered. What a terrible tragedy. *(She lies down on the ground, and scatters her body parts about the room.)*

JOHN. Oh, Lord, how will we ever stage this in a real production? We must hold auditions for an actress to play my wife, and see who can break up into different pieces and scatter themselves around the room. John Jr.! John the Second! Johnna! Come clean up your rooms, and gather your mother's body parts together. This is no way to live, with a tragedy strewn about the kitchen or living room this way like so many snap peas.

JOHNNA. *(Calling from the living room.)* I can't help, Daddy! I'm still tied to the grand piano leg, and I'm holding my enema water. May I please be untied and allowed to expel my water and then go live with my grandparents or something?

JOHN. You kids! You're just impossible. Here, let me beat you. *(John beats all three children to within an inch of their lives.)*

Stop crying, I'll give you something to cry about. *(Hits one of them.)*

There! That's something to cry about! *(Punches another one.)*

And *that's* something to cry about! Why aren't you crying? Did I knock the breath out of you? Well, good! I am a very angry man, and I am learning to express my anger. *(Punches and kicks them to the death.)*

Oh, Lord, now they're all dead. Oh, dear. Oh, my. Oh, well. *(To audience.)*

Sorry, I feel I've gotten dark again. Let me start over. My wife is not dead. I have not killed the children. We have not mentioned enemas or the movie *Sybil* or a murderous next-door neighbor named Tommy Psycho Babbit. *(To the pieces of Mary on the ground.)*

Come on, Mary, pull yourself together now. Stand up. None of this being in the dumps, spread around the room. *(The actress playing Mary reconstructs herself and becomes a whole, living person again.)*

We certainly were right to cast you, that was excellent! Mary, I love you.

MARY. ... nd ... ee ... uhb ... oooo, ... ohn.

JOHN. No, dear, the mouth's half hanging off your face, can you fix it? Ah, that's better. And I love you, Mary.

MARY. And I love you, John.

JOHN. Thank goodness we live in the fifties. We're safe here. The atom bomb may destroy the world in big blasts, following then with long, lingering radiation sickness. And there may be foreign communists in our midst, who are disguising themselves as Margaret Chase Smith and Adlai Stevenson, and who may take over our country and enslave us at any minute. But if those two things *don't* happen, then we will live very very happy lives together.

MARY. I'm very happy, John. I love you. Look at the ducky on the yard.

JOHN. Yes, a lovely ducky. I love you, Mary.

MARY. I'm happy.

JOHN. I'm happy, Mary. *(Mary's eye falls out.)* Pick it up, would you, Mary?

MARY. Sorry, John. *(Picks up eye, puts it back in socket.)*

JOHN. Well, let's go to bed. Before anything else falls apart. We'll try to bring the children back to life tomorrow. But I don't want anything else to go wrong tonight. So, hurry, let's go to sleep.

MARY. I made you a casserole, Mary.

JOHN. You're Mary.

MARY. I'm Mary. I love you, John.

JOHN. Fine. And I love you, Mary. And thanks for the casserole. We can microwave in the morning, if it won't cause cancer or make the whole goddamn house be riddled with radiation. Let's nap. Dr. Kevorkian is due shortly after 8 P.M. He's going to sell us some life insurance, and then make himself the beneficiary. And then we'll finally have rest.

MARY. Oh, I need to rest, I'm exhausted. I love you, John.

JOHN. I love you, Mary. *(They go to bed, exhausted. The house waits for the visit of Dr. Kevorkian.)*

AUTHOR'S NOTE

Afterword

Obviously this play asks for some physical things that it would be impossible to actually do.

I thought one solution would be to have someone onstage, disconnected from the characters, who simply read the stage directions aloud; and the actors could thus "indicate" the actions, without having to do them too full out. I also thought the reading of the sometimes gruesome directions would be a good distancing effect.

Director David Chambers and the talented actors at South Coast Rep came up with another solution that leaned heavily on the sound design (done by Garth Hemphill).

Whenever a gruesome effect occurred in the script — the one that reads "She lies down on the ground, and scatters her body parts about the room," for instance — we heard on the speaker system some horrific, though somewhat stylized sounds (of terrible ripping or tearing or unscrewing); and Amanda Carlin as the mother contorted her head and turned her neck, and then made her arm go limp and akimbo, and then made her leg go limp and akimbo, and then she lay down on the floor, dead. And the effect, amusingly and disturbingly, was as if we had seen her (sort of) be dismembered. When pages later, John told her to reconstruct herself, she did the same gestures, but in reverse.

So using sound and strange stage movement seems a very viable way to approach this piece. Don't go for trying to make it realistic or too gruesome; the ideas in the piece are gruesome enough, the audience needs that bit of distance to be able to bear it.

And for the actor playing John Doe, I intend that he have as much conversational charm and friendliness talking to the audience as possible — as if James Stewart or Steve Martin (in his good father movie roles) were playing the part; and that's how Hal Landon, Jr. did the part at South Coast. And thus his to-the-audience apologies are meant to be sincere (and do seem to help the piece from alienating the audience; right when they're about to be grossed out, the main character apologizes).

There may be other interpretations possible — such as playing John as more of a live wire waiting to explode (like a bottled-up Robert Duvall or Tommy Lee Jones, for instance). But the friendly, low-key approach I described above is what I envisioned, and is how Hal Landon, Jr. played it intuitively without any suggestions from me.

Well, good luck with it.

NOT MY FAULT

NOT MY FAULT was presented by the Theatre Workshop at the National Arts Club, in New York City, in December 1996. It was directed by Jeffrey D. Stocker, and the cast was as follows:

JACK..Sean Sullivan
MARGIE..Arloa Haythorn
SELINA ....Lynn Cohen
HARRY...Kevin Del Aquila

It was subsequently presented in February 1997 at Baruch College in New York City, as part of a psychology class. The cast was the same as above, except that HARRY was played by Michael Marchetta. And there was an earlier reading of the play that featured David Eigenberg as JACK, Crista Moore as MARGIE, Cynthia Darlow as SELINA, and Daniel Mastrogiorgio as HARRY.

AUTHOR'S NOTE

This short play was written specifically for a program geared to presenting plays about addiction to high school audiences. And one of the two performances at the National Arts Club was for a high school audience.

I became involved in this through winning a three-year writing fellowship from the Lila Wallace Readers Digest Fund. As a condition of the grant, a recipient is asked to do something out in the community that he or she might not do otherwise.

Because I come from a background with lots of alcoholism in it, and because I have spent a fair amount of time attending both Alanon and Adult Children of Alcoholics, I decided to do something on the issue of alcoholism.

My first year of the grant, connected with the Alcoholism Council of New York, I ran a writing workshop for people who came from alcoholic family backgrounds.

The first weekend of the workshop, however, was not about writing, but was an intensive workshop, run by therapist Sherrye Everett, which used a technique called "family sculpting."

Each member of the group was asked to create (or "sculpt") a living picture of his or her family of origin. This was done by a theatre game technique, using the other members of the group to stand in for and to "play act" as that person's parents, siblings and significant relatives.

Each member play-acting the person's family members was given three or four significant, familiar phrases which had been said frequently in the person's past — things like "you'll never amount to anything," "you're the reason I drink," "I'm just a social drinker," "you're worthless," "you're going to grow up like your drunk Aunt Sadie," etc., etc.

And then, armed with these incessant phrases, the play-actors were sort of "let loose" to improvise what would happen in that family, given the psychological cluster of unspoken rules, beliefs, angers, and resentments that these phrases reflected and grew out of.

And the participant whose family was being "sculpted" that way was asked to play his or her self.

This "family sculpting" weekend was extraordinarily powerful, though also exhausting and excruciatingly painful to watch and participate in. (It was also healing and worthwhile, but quite an experience, not something to be taken on lightly. It was also necessary to make sure the participants were far enough along in their recoveries to handle the emotions that would arise.)

On the weekends that followed this, I then ran a more conventional sort of writing workshop, though the topic of the work was meant to be alcoholism-related. My theory was that all the participants would write from a rawer, more connected place than they might have without the family sculpting exercise. (I also fully participated in the family sculpting exercise, and so was ready and willing to be in a raw space as well.)

Anyway, that was year one of my grant.

In the subsequent two years, I combined forces with Jeffrey Stocker who, supported by the Smithers Foundation, had been presenting staged readings of plays about addiction to high school students (and to college students at nearby Baruch College).

Stocker had expanded his work to a writers' workshop encouraging people to write plays specifically about addiction, and geared to being a springboard for discussion afterward. I and several of the writers from my workshop joined his group; and I eventually wrote this play, which was presented to a high school audience and also to two large psychology classes at Baruch College.

Alcoholism is very much a theme in my play THE MARRIAGE OF BETTE AND BOO (my one unabashedly biographical work, based more or less on my parents' marriage); and it features also in the more surreal BABY WITH THE BATHWATER.

For this play, knowing it was meant to trigger discussion, I feel I wrote about the topic a bit heavy-handedly (though purposely so).

It is primarily not a comedy, though in the hands of skilled actors, there is behavioral humor in the mother's preposterously large denial and avoidance of all problems, in the older brother's sarcasm and being fed up with the addicts in his family, and (though harder to play) in some of the wife's frustrations with her addict husband in the first scene.

So that's how this play came about.

CHARACTERS

JACK — late 20s, early 30s, likable, or can be, but takes responsibility for nothing, thinks everything is everybody else's fault.

MARGIE — late 20s, early 30s, Jack's ex-wife, nice, but really fed up with Jack.

SELINA — late 40s, early 50s (or older), Jack's mother, likes Jack, lives in a fuzzy haze most of the time; doesn't like the harshness of reality, wants to take the edge off of everything.

HARRY — mid to late 30s, Jack's older brother, very responsible, a bit of a nag, a bit self-righteous; on the other hand, he is accurate and more tied to reality than the rest of his family.

NOT MY FAULT

SCENE 1

Jack, Margie. They address the audience directly.

JACK. I am not an alcoholic. I mean, my wife'll come out here and tell you I am, but she's a bitch and she hates me for some reason I don't understand. I thought we were happy until she kicked me out three years ago.

MARGIE. Jack *is* an alcoholic. You don't drink beer at nine o'clock in the morning if you don't have a problem.

JACK. Look, you don't get drunk on beer. Or at least I don't. And I don't drink at nine in the morning. Well, a couple of times I did, but that was when I was up all night, partying, and so it wasn't drinking in the morning. It was really drinking late, late at night. And that's normal.

MARGIE. Nothing you do is normal.

JACK. Yeah, well you have a problem.

MARGIE. I got sick of it. He'd say he was comin' home after work, then he wouldn't show up, I'd have made dinner, our little boy wanted to see his father ...

JACK. Oh, get out the violins, why don't you?

MARGIE. Then he'd show up hours later, he'd stopped at some bar or other ...

JACK. Look, I stopped to buy a couple of six packs, this guy I know through my work — so it was work-related, bitch —

MARGIE. Don't call me a bitch.

JACK. Well, don't call me an alcoholic.

MARGIE. Fine. You're not an alcoholic. I'm a mental case. I just imagine you're drunk all the time.

JACK. That's right. Now you're finally making sense. So, I ran into Bobby, he works for Sony, they have a lot of stuff in our store, so it's business, and he says, why don't we go get a drink ... and what am I supposed to say? Oh, no, my wife wants me

135

home, I have a curfew, like I'm a teenager or something?

MARGIE.   I'm your ex-wife. And you're not as mature as a teenager. You're more like a five-year-old. Except our five-year-old is more mature than you.

JACK.   Fine. I'm worthless, you're perfect, is that how it is?

MARGIE.   Yes it is. Well, no it isn't. My therapist says I have to talk in "I" statements. I felt frightened when you didn't come home because you stopped at a bar. I feel frightened that if you get drunk, you'll lose your job.

JACK.   They like me at work.

MARGIE.   Why did they fire you then?

JACK.   I don't know why they fired me. They didn't fire me. I quit.

MARGIE.   Why did you quit?

JACK.   They weren't showing me enough respect. They weren't treating me right.

MARGIE.   Well, in what way?

JACK.   Look, we're not married anymore, I don't have to answer these fucking questions anymore. They didn't respect me, I spit in their face, I quit.

MARGIE.   People respect you when you do something worthy of respect. Not when you show up and act like a jerk.

JACK.   Oh, thanks a lot. Is that what you tell your son, your father is a jerk?

MARGIE.   No. I try to only say nice things about you. I say you have nice eyes. That we used to be happy.

JACK.   Well, that's great. Thanks a lot.

MARGIE.   You haven't paid child support in a year and a half.

JACK.   I don't have any money.

MARGIE.   Yeah. Well, you have a child. I have a job, I pay a full half of my salary for child care … but from you, nothing.

JACK.   What is this, the let's pick on Jack Show? I do my share. Last week, I took him out for a hot dog, did he tell you that?

MARGIE.   A hot dog costs a dollar.

JACK.   Yeah, well, when you have zero in the bank account, a dollar counts for a lot. I could have bought a beer with that dollar, but I didn't, I bought the kid a hot dog.

MARGIE.   Well, bully for you. We should award you the Nobel

Peace Prize.

JACK. You're a bitch.

MARGIE. You're a drunk and a bum.

JACK. I thought your therapist wanted you to talk only in "I" statements.

MARGIE. I ... feel you are a drunk and a bum.

JACK. And I feel you are a bitch. If you'd been nicer to me, maybe I wouldn't've drunk so much.

MARGIE. I thought you said you didn't drink.

JACK. I don't drink. I drink normal.

MARGIE. What's normal?

JACK. Look, 10 to 12 beers a day is normal.

MARGIE. It isn't. 10 to 12 Coca-Colas a day isn't normal.

JACK. What does Coca Cola have to do with anything?

MARGIE. Nothing. I just mean if you drink 10 or 12 of anything in a day, it suggests something is wrong.

JACK. So I'll drink water all day, is that what you want?

MARGIE. I don't want anything. I want you to get a job, and pay me some child support.

JACK. Okay, I'll get a job. Stop nagging me.

MARGIE. Why were you fired?

JACK. I wasn't fired. I quit.

MARGIE. Well, why did you quit, asshole? We need the money!

JACK. You call me an asshole again, I'm gonna break your face. *(They pause.)*

MARGIE. "I" statement. I feel frightened when you say you will break my face. I feel frightened when you don't have a job and can't pay child support. Although when you did have a job, last month, you didn't pay child support then either.

JACK. My car needed a new battery.

MARGIE. Oh shut up, get a job and pay me some child support. Or graduate to heroin and die of an overdose, and then I'll just forget about you. *(Exits.)*

JACK. I don't know what went wrong with our marriage. But she's just a bitch. I'm gonna go get a beer. *(Looks at audience.)* Look, it's four in the fuckin' afternoon, I've had a hard day, if I want a beer, it's no big deal. Jesus. *(Exits.)*

SCENE 2

Jack's mother, Selina. She's older. She sits in a chair. She is drinking a glass of white wine. She has a bottle of wine on the floor near her.

SELINA. Jack is my youngest son. He's really had a hard time of it. They don't treat him right at work, and his wife has, I don't know, I guess she's gone crazy. She's always going on about his drinking, like he has a problem or something.

But you know, I have a rule about how to tell if you have a problem. First of all: do you drink out of a glass? I only drink wine from a glass. I never drink directly from the bottle. So that's a very good sign that you don't have a problem, that you're just a social drinker.

I mean, life is difficult, and a little bit of wine or a highball never hurt anyone, and it sometimes makes it just a little bit easier to get through the day.

I mean, if you're falling down drunk in the gutter — you know, like a Bowery Bum or something — or if you get fired from your job because you're drunk or something ... well, then I think you may have a problem. But I never got fired from a job. Well, I never held a job. So I couldn't very well get fired. But no one has ever complained about my drinking.

Well, my daughter Judy does; and my son Harry does. But something is wrong with them. They're hyper-critical.

I think when they die, God will punish them for being so mean. And then God and I will share a highball and sit on a cloud and have a good ol' time.

But Jack never complained about my drinking, because he saw that I drank out of a glass. So Jack is really my favorite. *(Pours some more wine.)* And chardonnay is also my favorite. Very dry, very delicate. *(Jack appears on another part of the stage, holding a phone. Phone rings. His mother doesn't answer the phone immediately.)*

Hello? Is the phone ringing or am I hallucinating?
JACK.   Oh, answer the phone please ...
SELINA.   *(To audience.)* No, I'm just kidding. I might say some-

thing like that if I wasn't just a social drinker. *(Answers the phone.)* Hello?

JACK.   Hello, Mom.

SELINA.   Oh, Jack, hello. Dear, what time is it actually, is it morning or afternoon?

JACK.   It's afternoon. I hope you're not too buzzed to talk, are you, Mother?

SELINA.   Oh, Jack, darling, it's always so wonderful to hear your voice. How's that bitch wife of yours? Did anyone hit her with a car or anything?

JACK.   No, Margie's still alive. Mom, I need some help.

SELINA.   Oh, you're not going to talk about AA again, are you? Those people are a bunch of losers who like to complain and feel self-important. Your wife is wrong. You don't have a drinking problem.

JACK.   No, it's not about AA.

SELINA.   Well, that's good.

JACK.   I've been arrested. I need $3,000 bail. *(Long pause.)* Mom, are you there?

SELINA.   I'm sorry, dear, my mind wandered for a moment. You said something upsetting. Was it something Margie did?

JACK.   I've been arrested. I need bail money.

SELINA.   Uh huh. Oh, Jack darling, you poor thing. It's so awful. Are you uncomfortable in jail?

JACK.   Well, I want to get out.

SELINA.   What are you in prison for? I don't mean to be critical.

JACK.   My ex-boss told the police lies about me.

SELINA.   Oh, that's terrible. Well, you were right to quit there. They never valued you for your full worth. Oh God, how are you going to get a job if you can't use your past employers as a reference?

JACK.   What?

SELINA.   Nothing, I just felt discouraged for a moment. People are always picking on you, Jack. It makes me angry. They picked on me too. They pick on the sensitive ones, Jack, they make life hard for you. And you probably don't have any beer in prison, do you? Do you want me to send you a bottle of something?

JACK. Well, if you'd pay the bail, that would be better than a bottle.

SELINA.   The bail. It was … gosh, Jack, I don't have $3,000. I'll give you what I have, but I don't have $3,000. What about that bitch Margie? Her mother has money. Why don't they pay your bail? How do they expect you to pay child support if you're in prison?

JACK.   Margie hates me. I don't know why. She tells her mother lies about me.

SELINA.   I know she does, it's just terrible.

JACK.   Mom, what about Harry and Judy? Could you talk to them?

SELINA.   Well, dear, they're still angry you never paid them back that $10,000 you borrowed.

JACK.   That's not my fault.

SELINA.   I know it's not.

JACK.   I mean, I'm in jail. I don't belong here. I'm not violent, I'm not a criminal.

SELINA.   I know you're not. I'll work up the courage, and I'll call Harry and Judy. Maybe if I beg them and cry, they'll give in.

JACK.   I mean, they have savings. What are they saving for?

SELINA.   Well, probably for their families. Judy and Harry are so selfish, always buying things for their screaming kids. I hate noise. Is it noisy in prison, dear? I hope it isn't. What were we talking about?

JACK.   I want you to call up Harry and Judy and get bail for me so I can get outta here.

SELINA.   Oh yes, right. I'll do it right away. I'll call you back, dear.

JACK.   The number is 555-4400.

SELINA.   And don't be frightened, baby. It's not your fault, everything will be fine. I love you, Jack.

JACK.   Did you get the number?

SELINA.   Yes, dear. Something hundred. I'll call information. Or call me back after a bit. I love you, Jack.

JACK.   I love you, Mom. (*He hangs up. She starts to drink from*

*the bottle, realizes what she's doing, carefully pours the wine into a
glass.)*

SELINA.   Oh, God. Harry or Judy first. Harry has more
money, Harry. *(She dials the phone. Phone rings. Harry shows up on
another part of the stage, carrying a phone, maybe cellular. Harry is a
bit older than Jack. He's responsible, dependable, and fed up with his
mother and brother and with everyone you can't depend on.)*

HARRY.   Hello?

SELINA.   *(Pathetic voice.)* Hello, Harry.

HARRY.   Mother, I'm busy now, what do you want?

SELINA.   I just wanted to hear your voice.

HARRY.   Well, I'm here. Testing, testing. That's my voice. Does
it make you feel better?

SELINA.   You always make me feel better, Harry. You're my
dependable son. We all admire you.

HARRY.   That's very nice, Mother. How far into your cups are
you today?

SELINA.   Don't be mean. How's your wife. How are the two
children?

HARRY.   Three children. Judy has two children.

SELINA.   So many children. It's hard to keep track.

HARRY.   Why don't you line up some empty wine bottles and
put the children's names on them? To help you remember.

SELINA.   That's a good suggestion. Harry, dear, I'm afraid I'm
calling with a problem.

HARRY.   I can only talk a minute.

SELINA.   Well, it's about your brother.

HARRY.   I'm sick of hearing about Jack, Mom. He's a grown
man, it's not up to me or Judy, or you, to take care of him.

SELINA.   Well, Harry, that's very nice to say, but when people
get in trouble you help them. That's what family means.

HARRY.   I thought family was about drinking and screaming.

SELINA.   It's about that too. But it's also about helping out.

HARRY.   I gave Jack $6,000 five months ago, Judy gave him
four. That was supposed to get him out of a hole. Why didn't
it?

SELINA.   Well, I guess he fell back in the hole.

HARRY.   I have my own expenses. Look, if he has a creditor, he should face up to it and work out a pay back plan. If you just pay them a little bit a month, they're willing to wait. But if you're like Jack and you don't return the phone calls and you never make any arrangements, well they get angry.

SELINA.   Oh, you're so proud of yourself, aren't you? So proud you pay your bills. Well, big fucking deal.

HARRY.   Thanks for calling, Mother. It's lovely to hear from you. *(Hangs up.)*

SELINA.   Oh God. Harry, Harry! *(She redials; phone rings.)*

HARRY.   *(Answers.)* What?

SELINA.   I'm sorry I lost my temper. I'm just kind of upset here.

HARRY.   Mother, are you calling about something specific?

SELINA.   Yes. Jack is in jail. We have to pay the bail. It's $3,000.

HARRY.   What is he in jail for?

SELINA.   Ummmm … *(Realizes she doesn't know.)* … ummmm, something. Some lie his employer told about him.

HARRY.   Mother, they don't put you in jail for some lie somebody tells.

SELINA.   Well, when you're unjustly accused they do. Don't you watch TV movies? People's lives can be ruined.

HARRY.   Jack's employer did not go to the police and say Jack is a bad person, put him in prison. They had to say something *specific;* and if Jack was put in jail, there must be some evidence or reason to believe what they said.

SELINA.   *(Filled with hate of Harry.)* Oh, you're so logical, why don't you just become president?

HARRY.   So Jack called you from prison, and you didn't even ask why he was there. Weren't you interested?

SELINA.   I love my son, and I know whatever he did, he had a reason for.

HARRY.   So if he robbed a bank and shot people, you'd forgive him.

SELINA.   I offer my son unconditional love.

HARRY.   That's interesting. You offer it to the one in trouble, but not to your other children.

SELINA.   The one in trouble needs my help.

HARRY.   Well, if he's in prison, he needs a lawyer. And we have to know what he's in prison for. Is it parking tickets? Did he kill someone? Did he steal something?

SELINA.   You always believe the worst of your brother.

HARRY.   Well, he's in prison. What am I supposed to think?

SELINA.   I don't know. I don't want to have to deal with these problems. Just get him out, would you? *(Hangs up; looks at her near empty bottle.)* I need another bottle. *(She scuffles off, carrying her bottle.)*

SCENE 3

Jack comes out to talk to the audience.

JACK.   Look, if you have to know, I hocked some VCRs from the store.

It's not that big of a deal, and I was going to return them when I got some money to get them out of hock.

So it wasn't really stealing, if I was going to pay them back.

You know, one of my jobs at the store is to repair VCRs, and people bring them in, and sometimes they leave them there for months, and I really needed some money.

I was seeing this girl, she was real hot, and she liked to smoke crack.

I mean, I'd never done it, and people seem to really like it. I mean, they like it so much they become prostitutes in the street in order to buy it, so it must be pretty powerful.

I mean, I'm not a crack addict, I only tried it a few times. And I was supposed to get a raise at my job, I work fucking hard for them; and instead when they found out I'd taken these VCRs out of the store and taken them to a pawnshop, they fired me.

So that's a big help.

Now I can't earn the money to get the fucking things out of hock.

So it's really not my fault. I mean, if they paid more, I wouldn't have had to hock the stuff, right?

And the stupid thing is they found one of the pawn tickets,

and it has my fingerprints on it, and so I can't say that I didn't take the VCRs. I mean, I can say it, but I don't think they're gonna believe me.

So I don't know. It's not that serious a crime, and they don't know about the crack thing.

And really I'm just on beer and tequila now, so I'm not a crack addict ...

It's real addictive, everything they tell you about it being hard to kick is true.

But I don't have money to buy it now anyway, and I want to earn money to pay child support, I love my kid, I'm a good father, I ... I just don't know how my life got to be here. *(Resentful.)* But I know if my wife was nicer to me, and if my brother wasn't such a tight ass, they'd get me outta here. But so far, they're just leaving me in this fuckin' place. *(Jack moves away and stops addressing the audience.)*

SCENE 4

Two simultaneous phone calls, meant to overlap.

On one part of the stage, Harry will speak with Margie. On another part of the stage, Jack calls up his mother Selina.

First, Harry dials his phone. Margie's phone rings. She answers it.

MARGIE. Hello.
HARRY. Hey, Margie. It's Harry.
MARGIE. *(With some dread; he only calls with serious topics.)* Oh, hello, Harry.
HARRY. I thought I better tell you that Jack is in jail.
MARGIE. What's he in jail for?
HARRY. My drunk of a mother didn't even ask him. I got the police report, it says he stole five VCRs from the store and he pawned them, and they have his fingerprints on one of the pawn tickets.

MARGIE. But why did he do that? I mean, he had a paying job ... if he steals from them, of course he'll be fired.

HARRY. Well, you expect my brother to use his brain?

MARGIE. But what did he use the money for? He didn't give any to me. I think he owes his rent. I think his car is broken. What did he use the money for?

HARRY. I don't know. Does he take drugs now too, do you think?

MARGIE. I didn't think he did. He used to smoke grass a lot, but ... well, I don't know what he used it for. But if he's taking something, I don't want Jimmy staying with him anymore. I don't want him to have visitation rights.

HARRY. Well ... (*Harry and Margie freeze when necessary, or try to fill the pauses needed by thinking, or turning upstage briefly. It's a theatrical convention; try to keep the conversations intercutting as best you can. During Margie's speech above, Jack dials, using the phone in jail. Selina's phone rings, she answers it.*)

JACK. Hello, Mom.

SELINA. (*Oozing sudden affection.*) Jack, baby.

HARRY. Well, visitation rights would be up to the Judge.

MARGIE. I mean, I haven't been worried about Jimmy before, but ...

JACK. Did Harry say he'd get me the money?

SELINA. How are you, baby?

HARRY. Well, we don't know he's taking anything. We're just guessing.

JACK. Mom, did you get the money?

SELINA. Oh, baby. (*Cries.*) Your brother is a bad brother.

MARGIE. Oh God, how did I ever hook up with somebody this much of a mess?

JACK. You didn't get it?
SELINA. He's mad about the other money you owe him, sweetie.

JACK. But I'm his brother. He's not going to leave me stuck in here.

JACK. I'm not a criminal.
SELINA. I know you're not, baby.

SELINA. Oh he seems to want to know what you're in prison for. I told him you didn't know.
JACK. What did you tell him that for? I know what I'm in prison for.
SELINA. Well, that's good, dear. As long as you know.

HARRY. I don't know. I can't stand my brother. You must have liked him for some reason. I never understood it.

MARGIE. Well, you don't have to be that hard on him. He has his nice points. He's fun at parties.

HARRY. On his gravestone, it can read: Partied well. Liked other people to pay his bills.

MARGIE. I feel sort of bad for him in jail. He hasn't been in prison before.

HARRY. Well, maybe he'll learn the consequences of his actions.

146

MARGIE. He hasn't learned it so far. I don't see why this would be any different.

JACK. Don't you want to know what I'm in jail for?
SELINA. I know whatever you did, it wasn't your fault.
JACK. That's right. It wasn't my fault.

MARGIE. *(Softening.)* You know, I could ask my mother for the bail money. My mother hates Jack, but I could ask her.
HARRY. Look, maybe leaving him in jail for a while will teach him a lesson.

JACK. Mom, is there anywhere you can get the money?
SELINA. I don't know ...

MARGIE. I wonder how bad jail is. I mean, Jack isn't violent. Won't he be around violent people?

JACK. What about your friend Harriet?
SELINA. I think she's dead, dear. Jack, I have to go.

HARRY. You know, feeling sorry for him doesn't really help him.

SELINA. This bottle is empty, I have to hope and pray I have something else in the liquor cabinet.

MARGIE. I know, but....

JACK. Mom, just get me out of here. I swear I'll get my life together.

SELINA. *(Fondly.)* You don't have to get your life together to please me, Jack. I love you no matter what kind of mess your life is.

JACK. *(Irony to himself.)* Thanks, Mom. That makes me feel good.

MARGIE. I'm starting to think of him there, and really, I mean ... don't most people make bail? I mean, he'll still have a trial, or plea bargain or something.

HARRY. You want to do this again?

JACK. Mom, are you still there?

SELINA. Yes, dear, but I have to go, I think.

HARRY. Okay, call your mother if you want to. I don't think I'm going to put up the bail. He might skip town and then you lose the money.

MARGIE. It can't all be about money. It's about people too.

JACK. Don't hang up yet.

HARRY. I'm sick of pouring money into him. He's a bad investment. He's not getting his life together.

SELINA. I feel a little dizzy. Maybe a sip of something.

JACK. It's scary here, Mom.
SELINA. Oh, baby. I don't wanna hear it. It upsets me.

JACK. Mom.

SELINA. I have to go, dear. Tomorrow's another day. Call me, dear, if you can.
JACK. I can't always use the phone here.
SELINA. Good-bye, dear. I hear something calling me from the liquor cabinet. You're never alone when you have a good drink. Love you, Jack. *(Hangs up; wanders off.)*
JACK. Love you, Mom. *(To himself.)* It's not my fault. None of it's my fault. *(Lights dim on him in jail. End.)*

MARGIE. I know, but maybe this'll shake him up, and he'll ... you know, seek help or something.

HARRY. He's never gonna get help. I'm sorry if I seem cold-hearted, I'm just sick of helping my brother, that's all. But if you haven't had enough of it yet, well, go to it.
MARGIE. I'm going to hang up now. Good-bye, Harry.

HARRY. Good-bye, Margie. *(Harry and Margie hang up, they both exit.)*

PROPERTY LIST

Glass of white wine (SELINA)
Bottle of white wine (SELINA)
Telephones (JACK, SELINA, HARRY, MARGIE)

THE HARDY BOYS
AND THE MYSTERY OF WHERE
BABIES COME FROM

THE HARDY BOYS AND THE MYSTERY OF WHERE BABIES COME FROM was first produced by New Mercury Group at Dixon Place, in New York City, on February 24–26, 1997, with three plays written by Craig Lucas, Perry Laylon Ojeda and Lanford Wilson. The evening was produced and directed by Randy Gener; the lighting and sound designs were by Yossi Wanono; the costume design was by Moira L. Shaughnessy; the projection design was by Joe E. Jeffreys and Randy Gener; the prop manager was Ellen Esposito; and the production stage manager was Bob Speck. The cast was as follows:

TV ANNOUNCER'S VOICE..........................Jordan Schildcraut
FRANK HARDY...John-Michael Lander
JOE HARDY ....Sam Trammell
NURSE RATCHED..Mike Jefferson
MR. HARDY.....................................Michael Edward O'Connor

This production was remounted at LaMama, Etc. with the same cast, except for Sam Trammell, who was unavailable and who was replaced by Matthew Vipond.

THE HARDY BOYS was also done as part of MIX AND MATCH DURANG at the John Drew Theatre, in East Hampton, New York, in 1997, directed by Elizabeth Gottlieb, with Jonathan Walker as FRANK HARDY, Michael Ian Black as JOE HARDY, Jennifer Van Dyck as NURSE RATCHED, and Peter Jacobson as MR. HARDY.

AUTHOR'S NOTE

Back when I wrote this sketch (in the late '70s), THE HARDY BOYS was a series on television, featuring cute Shaun Cassidy and cute Parker Stevenson, looking preppy and wearing sweaters.

The title was actually given to me by my friend Stephen Paul Davis. Thank you, Stephen.

I find myself tempted to write 22 more episodes of these Hardy Boys, but then there is an awful lot of other things I should be doing with my life too, aren't there? Other Hardy Boy episodes is perhaps a low priority. Or is it?

CHARACTERS

FRANK HARDY, a cute young man
JOE HARDY, another cute young man
NURSE RATCHED, a terrifying nurse
MR. HARDY, Frank and Joe's father

THE HARDY BOYS AND THE MYSTERY OF WHERE BABIES COME FROM

SCENE 1

Scene: The Hardy Boys' bedroom. Bunk beds. Posters on the wall.

If possible, a screen upstage that has titles from time to time. (This can also be done with a voice over the speaker system if you prefer.) At the top of play on the screen we see the title: THE HARDY BOYS AND THE MYSTERY OF WHERE BABIES COME FROM.

Music plays underneath the title. (Somewhat ominous mystery music, mixed with weekly dramatic TV series music.)

Frank Hardy sits at his desk. He is around age 20, nice looking, preppy, wearing a collegiate sweater.

Joe Hardy, his brother, comes in. He's around age 20, nice looking, preppy, wearing a collegiate sweater.

JOE.   Hi, Frank.
FRANK.   Hi, Joe.
JOE.   Neat sweater, Frank.
FRANK.   Yours too, Joe.
JOE.   Dad gave me mine.
FRANK.   He gave me mine too.
JOE.   Dad's great.
FRANK.   Yeah, he is. Great.
JOE.   You wanna play Monopoly?
FRANK.   Not now.
JOE.   Chess?

FRANK. No, you have to think too hard.

JOE. Clue?

FRANK. No, but you're getting closer. Why don't we do some sleuthing?

JOE. Oooh, I love the word "sleuthing," Frank. It makes me feel excited right in the pit of my stomach.

FRANK. Me too. It's a great word.

JOE. Is there some mystery to solve, Frank, that we can use our sleuthing powers on?

FRANK. Yes, Joe, there is. But let's change sweaters first. *(Lights change, dimmer. Music. We watch Frank and Joe put on different sweaters. Then on the screen [or on the loudspeaker] A FEW MINUTES LATER. Lights come back up, full, on the bedroom. The boys regard their different sweaters.)*

JOE. Nice sweater, Frank.

FRANK. Yours too, Joe.

JOE. Now what's the mystery?

FRANK. Well I heard someone at school say that Nancy Drew may have to get married because "she has a bun in the oven." *(They both look baffled.)*

JOE. Gosh, Frank, that doesn't make any sense at all. Our housekeeper Mrs. Danvers has had whole cakes in the oven, and she's never had to get married.

FRANK. That's just it. Something's fishy here.

JOE. *(Shudders pleasurably.)* I love the word "fishy." It makes me feel excited right in the pit of my stomach.

FRANK. Me too, Joe. And you're right — this whole thing *doesn't* make sense. Let me think. *(Thinks.)* No, it hurts.

JOE. Well how shall we solve this mystery? I know — let me interrogate you! Frank, who told you this crazy thing about "buns in the oven"?

FRANK. I don't remember.

JOE. Well, that finishes that investigation.

FRANK. No — wait. The school nurse said it!

JOE. Nurse Ratched! *(Sound of ominous music.)* Gosh, that music sure is ominous. I wish Mrs. Danvers would leave our stereo system alone. Maybe we can get Dad to fire her. Then it would be just guys living in the house. I'd prefer that. *(The omi-*

nous music fades out.)

FRANK. Me too. At least she doesn't sleep here.

JOE. And she's so crazy. Always trying to get me to jump out the window.

FRANK. That's just her sense of humor.

JOE. Well, I don't find it funny. Women are terrifying, aren't they?

FRANK. That's what Dad always said.

JOE. Say, speaking of terrifying women, maybe we should go see Nurse Ratched and ask her what she meant about all this bun in the oven stuff.

FRANK. We *could* ask her, but that seems too simple.

JOE. Why don't we do some *sleuthing* then? *(Shudders with delight.)* Oooooh, my stomach again. It's just like late at night when I ... well, never mind. Why don't we go see Nurse Ratched, but we won't actually ask her anything, we'll pretend we're sick, and we'll kinda talk around things listening for clues, and that way it'll still be *sleuthing!* Oooooooh!

FRANK. That's a good idea, Joe. But let's change sweaters first.

JOE. Ok. *(As the lights fade and series music plays, the boys start to take off their sweaters. On the screen we see: END OF EPISODE ONE.)*

SCENE 2

The stage changes (or lights shift) to the School Nurse's office.

Nurse Ratched is there, looking through the men's underwear section of the Sears Roebuck catalog.

On the screen we see: EPISODE TWO.

Frank and Joe come in, wearing new sweaters.

FRANK. Hello, Nurse Ratched.

NURSE RATCHED. Well, hello, boys. Nice sweaters. What can I do you for?

JOE. We wanted to ask you a que ... *(Frank jabs him in the ribs.)*

FRANK. One of us is sick. We think it might be strep throat.

NURSE RATCHED. Strep throat, huh? Which one of you has it?

JOE. We're not sure. We thought you better examine both of us.

NURSE RATCHED. Sure, I'll examine you. Oh, you boys are so cute, I could eat you up!

FRANK. Eat us up ... like "buns in the oven?"

NURSE RATCHED. No, not like buns in the oven. Like hot dogs! *(Laughs hysterically.)*

JOE. Gee, another terrifying woman whose sense of humor I don't understand.

NURSE RATCHED. Now which of you is Frank, and which of you is Joe, I get confused.

FRANK. I'm Frank.

JOE. And I'm Joe.

NURSE RATCHED. And I'm ready for action. *(Laughs hysterically.)* Oh I'm going to be fired if I don't watch it. I just love young men. That's why I took this job. All right, boys, take your shirts and pants off, I want to look at your throats.

JOE. Ok, but you gotta promise that you'll talk some more about buns in the oven.

NURSE RATCHED. Sure. Hot cross buns, French pastries, French movies, X-rated X-rays. Anything you want, Joe.

JOE. Frank.

NURSE RATCHED. I thought you said you were Joe.

JOE. Oh, I'm sorry, I am Joe. I just got confused.

FRANK. You bozo.

NURSE RATCHED. Ok, boys, now take off your clothes. *(Ominous music. The boys start to remove their sweaters. Lights out on them. On the screen we see a picture of a large clock, which is at three o'clock. This picture of the clock fades into the same clock, later, at 7:15. Lights come back on the Nurse's office. The lighting suggests twilight a bit, maybe has some orange coming in from the side. Frank and Joe are in t-shirts and boxer shorts, tied up back-to-back on the examining table. They are alone.)*

FRANK. I didn't know they had to tie you up to check for

strep throat.

JOE. Neither did I.

FRANK. Okay, let's add up the facts we know so far about the mystery.

JOE. Well, Nurse Ratched says we don't have hernias because she gave us that coughing test for two hours.

FRANK. All right, that's fact number one. What else?

JOE. Well, she thinks we're cute.

FRANK. I think we're cute too, but we need more clues than that to solve this mystery. Nancy may be in trouble!

JOE. I find it hard to think all bundled up this way. I wonder when Nurse Ratched is coming back with the bicycle pump? *(Mr. Hardy, Frank and Joe's father, comes into the Nurse's office, wearing a suit and looking annoyed.)*

MR. HARDY. Frank, Joe! What are you two boys doing here all tied up?

FRANK. We're sleuthing, Dad.

JOE. Ooooo-oooooooh.

MR. HARDY. You two boys really are retarded. I should have my sperm analyzed. Don't you know that Nurse Ratched is a sex maniac?

JOE. Gosh, Dad, no! Is she?

FRANK. Wow. And what's sperm?

JOE. And what's sex, and what's maniac, and what's retarded?

FRANK. And why should Nancy have to get married because of some breakfast food she has in her oven?

MR. HARDY. What? Breakfast food?

FRANK. There must be some reason she has to get married.

MR. HARDY. She's pregnant. *(Joe and Frank look at one another, astonished.)*

FRANK. Pregnant!

JOE. Gosh!

FRANK. What's pregnant?

MR. HARDY. Well, I guess you boys are old enough to be told the facts now. I kinda wanted to wait until you were 35 or so, but maybe now that you already know this much, I better tell you the rest. Ok, fellas, listen up. I'm about to explain where babies come from.

JOE.   Babies! What do babies have to do with buns in the oven?

MR. HARDY.   Well, it's complicated, and a little bit disgusting.

FRANK.   Go ahead, Dad, we can take it.

MR. HARDY.   We'll start with the flower and the bee. The bee pollinates the flower, by taking pollen from the stamen, and delivering it to the pistil, which in the human species is like fertilizing the egg, which is … *(Nurse Ratched appears behind Mr. Hardy and puts a cloth soaked in chloroform over his mouth.)*

NURSE RATCHED.   That's about all the filth I think the boys should learn today, Mr. Hardy. *(Mr. Hardy falls to the floor.)*

JOE.   Gosh, Dad, you've been chloroformed. *(To Nurse Ratched.)* Why did you do that? Are you crazy?

NURSE RATCHED.   Is the Pope Catholic?

JOE.   I don't know. He's Polish. Is he Catholic too?

FRANK.   Wait, Joe, we got some clues from Dad right before he lost consciousness. He said something about eggs, and you make eggs on *top* of the oven, while you make buns *inside* of the oven. Maybe there's some clue about being on top, and being inside.

JOE.   It doesn't ring any bells with me, Frank. I think we have a lot more *sleuthing* to do, ooooo-oooooh.

NURSE RATCHED.   Something make you shiver, honey?

FRANK.   The bee, the flower. Inside, on top.

NURSE RATCHED.   That's very nice. That's almost a haiku.

JOE.   Hi coo? Gosh, I just don't understand women.

NURSE RATCHED.   That's 'cause we have different hormones.

JOE.   I heard about that in health class. We had to do a paper on what makes a hormone.

NURSE RATCHED.   And what makes a hormone?

JOE.   I don't know. I got an F. Is that a good grade?

NURSE RATCHED.   Oh, I like a good F.

FRANK.   Can you go away for a minute? I need to think.

NURSE RATCHED.   Well, I'll be right back, and then we'll take some pictures. *(She leaves.)*

FRANK.   I'm so confused. I feel we're on the brink of learning a really big mystery, but I'm finding it hard to concentrate

160

because we're all tied up in our underwear, and that crazy woman keeps coming in here acting all funny.

JOE.   But she said she wasn't crazy. She said she was a Polish Catholic.

FRANK.   I don't know. *(Sees something, tense.)* Joe, look! *(Frank and Joe look over to a corner, where their sweaters lie in a heap.)* Joe. She didn't even fold our sweaters!

JOE.   Gosh.

FRANK.   Joe — I think maybe she *is* crazy. *(Ominous music. On the screen we see: END OF EPISODE TWO. Then we see: NEXT WEEK FRANK AND JOE JOIN A HEALTH CLUB AND GET A FUNGUS IN A STRANGE PLACE. Music finishes. End of play.)*

PROPERTY LIST

Chloroform soaked cloth (NURSE RATCHED)

MEDEA

(Co-authored with Wendy Wasserstein)

MEDEA was co-written by Chris Durang and Wendy Wasserstein for the Juilliard School's Drama Division's 25th anniversary, April 25th, 1994 at the Juilliard Theater, New York City. The evening was produced by Margot Harley. It was directed by Gerald Gutierrez; the choreography was by Christopher Chadman; and the musical direction was by Tom Fay. The cast for the evening consisted of many Juilliard graduates. For this particular sketch the cast was as follows:

MEDEA .... Harriet Harris
THE CHORUS .. Laura Linney, Diane Venora, Denise Woods
JASON .... Kevin Spacey
MESSENGER.. Randle Mell
ANGEL EX MACHINA .... David Schramm

CHARACTERS

MEDEA, an angry woman
THE CHORUS, the chorus
JASON, Medea's husband
MESSENGER
ANGEL

MEDEA

The actress who is to play Medea comes out and makes the following introduction.

ACTRESS. Hello. I am she who will be Medea. That is, I shall play the heroine from that famous Greek tragedy by Euripides for you.

I attended a first rate School of Dramatic Arts. At this wonderful school, I had classical training, which means we start at the very beginning, a very good place to start. Greek tragedy. How many of you in the audience have ever acted in Greek tragedy? How many of your lives are Greek tragedy? Is Olympia Dukakis here this evening?

As an actress who studied the classics, one of the first things you learn in drama school is that there are more roles for men than for women. This is a wonderful thing to learn because it is true of the real world as well. Except for *Thelma and Louise.* At drama school, in order to compensate for this problem, the women every year got to act in either *The Trojan Women* or *The House of Bernardo Alba.* This prepared us for bit parts on *Designing Women* and *Little House on the Prairie.* Although these shows are cancelled now, and we have nothing to do.

Tonight, we would like to present to you a selection from one of the most famous Greek tragedies ever written, *The Trojan Women.* Our scene is directed by Michael Cacoyannis and choreographed by June Taylor. And now, translated from the Greek by George Stephanoulous, here is a scene from this terrifying tragedy. *(Names the cast members:)* (N) _____, (N) _____ and (N) _____ will play the Chorus. (N) _____ and (N) _____ will play the men. *(Dramatically.)*

And I, (N)_____, will play Medea. *(The actress playing Medea exits with purpose and panache. Enter the three actresses who play the Chorus. They are dressed in togas. Most of the time they speak in unison. Sometimes they speak solo lines. In the style of the piece, they are over-dramatic and over-wrought. But most of the time they should act their lines as if they are the words from genuine Greek tragedy, full of intonation and emotional feeling. Don't send them up, or wink at the audience. Let the juxtaposition of Greek tragedy acting style and the sometimes silly lines be what creates the humor.)*

CHORUS. *(In unison.)*

So pitiful, so pitiful
your shame and lamentation.
No more shall I move the shifting pace
of the shuttle at the looms of Ida.

CHORUS MEMBER #3. *(Echoes.)*

Looms of Ida.

CHORUS.

Can you not, Queen Hecuba, stop this Bacchanal before
her light feet whirl her away into the Argive camp?

CHORUS MEMBER #3. *(Echoes.)*

Argive camp.

CHORUS. *(In unison.)*

O woe, o woe, o woe,
We are so upset we speak in unison,
So pitiful, so wretched, so doomed,
Women who run with wolves
Women who love too much,
Whitewater rapids, how did she turn $1000 into $100,000?
O woe, o woe, o woe.
Here she comes now.
Wooga, wooga, wooga.

(Enter Medea in a dramatic, blood red toga. She is in high, excessive grief and fury.)

MEDEA.

Come, flame of the sky,
Pierce through my head!
What do I, Medea, gain from living any longer?
Oh I hate living! I want
to end my life, leave it behind, and die.

CHORUS. *(In unison; chanted seriously.)*

But tell us how you're really feeling.

MEDEA. My husband Jason — the Argonaut — has left me for another woman. Debbie.

CHORUS. *(In unison.)*
    Dreaded Debbie, dreaded Debbie.
    Debutante from hell.
MEDEA. She is the daughter of King Creon, who owns a diner on 55th Street and Jamaica Avenue. Fie on her! And the House of Creon! And the four brothers of the Acropolis.

    I am banished from my husband's bed, and from the country. A bad predicament all around. But I am skilled in poison. Today three of my enemies I will strike down dead: Debbie and Debbie's father and my husband.
CHORUS. *(In unison.)*
    Speaking of your husband, here he comes.
(Enter Jason, dressed in a toga, but also with an armored breast plate and wearing a soldier's helmet with a nice little red adornment on top. Sort of like a costume from either Ben Hur *or* Cleopatra. *He perhaps is not in the grand style, but sounds more normal and conversational.)*
JASON. Hello, Medea.
MEDEA. Hello, Jason.
JASON. I hear you've been banished to China.
MEDEA. *(Suddenly Noel Coward brittle.)* Very large, China.
JASON. And Japan?
MEDEA. Very small, Japan. And Debbie?
JASON. She's very striking.
MEDEA. Some women should be struck regularly like gongs.
JASON. Medea, even though thou art banished by Creon to foreign shores, the two innocent children of our loins, Lyle and Erik, should remain with me. I will enroll them at the Dalton School. And there will they will flourish as citizens of Corinth under the watchful eye of Zeus and his lovely and talented wife Hera.
MEDEA. Fine, walk on me some more! I was born unlucky and a woman.
CHORUS. *(In unison.)*
    Men are from Mars, women are from Venus.
JASON. Well, whatever. I call the gods to witness that I have done my best to help you and the children.
MEDEA. Go! You have spent too long out here. You are consumed with craving for your newly-won bride, Debbie. Go,

enjoy Debbie! *(Jason shrugs, exits.)* O woe, o woe. I am in pain for I know what I must do. Debbie, kill for sure.

CHORUS. *(In unison.)*

> Debbie's done, ding dong, Debbie's done.
>
> Done deal, Debbie dead.
>
> Dopey Debbie, Debbie dead.

MEDEA.   But also my sons. Never shall their father see them again. I shall kill my children. *(Ferociously, to the Chorus.)* How do you like that????

CHORUS. *(In unison.)*

> Aaaaaaagghghghghghghggghhhhh!
>
> O smart women, foolish choices.
>
> Stop the insanity! Stop the insanity!
>
> You can eat one slice of cheese, or 16 baked potatoes!
>
> Make up your mind.

MEDEA.   Why is there so little *Trojan Women* in this, and so much of me?

CHORUS. *(In unison.)*

> We don't know *The Trojan Women* as well as we know *Medea.* *(Spoken, not sung.)*
>
> Medea, we just met a girl named Medea.
>
> And suddenly that name
>
> Will never be the same.

MEDEA.   Bring my children hither.

CHORUS. *(In unison.)*

> O miserable mother, to destroy your own increase, murder the babes of your body. The number you have reached is not in service at this time. Call 777-FILM.

MEDEA.   *(In a boiling fury.)* I want to kill my children. I want to sleep with my brother. I want to pluck out the eyes of my father. I want to blow up the Parthenon. I need a creative outlet for all this anger. *(Enter the Messenger, carrying a head. He kneels before Medea.)*

MESSENGER.   I am a messenger. Caesar is dead.

CHORUS. *(In unison.)*

> Caesar is dead. How interesting. Who is Caesar?

MESSENGER.   I am sorry. Wrong message. *(Reads from piece of*

paper.) Lady Teazle wishes you to know that Lady Windermere and Lady Bracknell are inviting you and Lady The-Scottish-Play to tea with her cousin Ernest, if he's not visiting Mr. Bunberry.
MEDEA. Mr. Bunberry? I do not need a messenger. I need a deus ex machina. *(Elaborate music. Enter an Angel with great big wings. Descending from the ceiling, or revealed on a balcony. Or dragging a step ladder that he stands on. Very dramatic whatever he does.)*
ANGEL. O Medea, O Medea.

I am a deus ex machina.
In a bigger production, I would come down from the sky in an angel's outfit, but just use your imagination. Theatre is greatly about imagination, is it not.

I am an angel.

I I I I I I I, yi yi yi.

I I I I am the Bird of Greek Tragedy.

Do not kill your children. Do not sleep with your brother. Rein in your rage, and thank Zeus. I come with glad tidings. Debbie is no more a threat. She's been cast in a series. She has a running part on *Home Improvements.*
CHORUS. *(In unison.)*

Home Improvements.
ANGEL. Jason will return to you. He sees the error of his ways. He has been lobotomized.
CHORUS. *(In unison.)*

O fortunate woman, to whom Zeus has awarded a docile
husband.
MEDEA. O, deus ex machina, o, angel:

O, Hecuba, oh, looms of Ida.
CHORUS. *(In unison.)*

Ida Ida Ida Ida.
MEDEA. I am eternally grateful to you.
CHORUS. *(In unison.)*

The things we thought would happen do not happen.

The unexpected, God makes possible.
(Spoken, not sung.)

The camptown races sing a song,

Do da, do da.

CHORUS and MEDEA. *(Switch to singing now.)*
Medea's happy the whole day long,
Oh the do da day!
Things will be just fine,
Things will be just great
No need to kill her children now,
Oh the do da ...
(Big musical coda:)
Oh the do da,
Zeus and Buddha,
They're as nice as
Dionysus,
Oh the do da
Work it though da
Oh the do da, do da, do da Day!
(Medea and the Chorus and the Angel strike a happy and triumphant pose.)

PROPERTY LIST

Piece of paper (MESSENGER)

AUTHOR'S NOTE

Afterword

I co-wrote this sketch with Wendy Wasserstein for a celebration of the Juilliard School's 25th anniversary of the Drama Division in spring of 1994.

Wendy and I went to Yale School of Drama together. And so why were they asking us to write a benefit for Juilliard? Well, Juilliard didn't have a playwriting program until 1993, so why not ask us, I guess.

My third year at Yale was Wendy's first year. Wendy and I became laughing pals together. We crammed for Theatre History exams the night before by using insane pneumonic devices. We drove to the New Haven airport together for milkshakes. We spent a New Year's together, drinking champagne and eating an entire mocha cake. (We both like sugar. And cake. And icing.) We liked and encouraged each other's writing.

Wendy and I have written together twice — a cabaret show at Yale (WHEN DINAH SHORE RULED THE EARTH) and a screenplay (HOUSE OF HUSBANDS) out in the real world. And then we have written two benefits together, including this recent one for Juilliard.

Our assignment for Juilliard was to write something about classical theatre. At first we were going to do something about THE TROJAN WOMEN. But Diana Rigg in MEDEA was playing on Broadway, so Wendy and I went to that, and then we wrote this.

The opening spoken introduction was geared a bit to the Juilliard alumni audience, and you could just cut it, if you think that's better. I included it here (with specific Juilliard references removed) because I thought the playful tone of it, and the "discussion" of classical theatre and its sometimes limited opportunities for women actresses, might be a useful way to help the audience situate themselves and know what to expect.

The part of Medea, obviously, calls for larger-than-life, proclamatory acting, but with a comic flair. And the Chorus can be tricky ... they should be as much like a Greek chorus as possible, speaking in unison when indicated; their tone should be dramatic and tragic, even when the words are silly. Too much "winking" in the tone of voice for the Chorus is less funny than letting it sound "straighter." Beyond that, your own sense of timing and comic flair will be your best guide.

I chose the silly "Camptown Races" song because that is in the public domain. I like the song to start recited, as if it's more Greek poetry, and then turn into song, as if the lyrics push the chorus along, sort of forcing them to burst into melody.

Wendy and I enjoyed writing this, and hope you have fun with it.

AUNT DAN MEETS THE MADWOMAN OF CHAILLOT

AUTHOR'S NOTE

I think you have to know Wallace Shawn's play AUNT DAN AND LEMON for this parody to make any sense at all. In case you don't, I'll tell you a bit about it.

Shawn's play was done at the Public Theatre in 1985. It presented a friendship between Lemon, a sickly girl, and her Aunt Dan (played by Linda Hunt). Aunt Dan is quite a character. She can't stop talking, she talks on and on and on, telling her opinions about how great Kissinger was and how right he was about the war in Vietnam, and how people who criticized him just did nothing to protect the quality of their life, but he went out there and was willing to act, to have people be killed, to protect what was comfortable in our society.

I'm partial to Shawn's writing. I met him when I auditioned for and got cast in an odd play of his called THE HOTEL PLAY at Cafe LaMama. And I loved his play MARIE AND BRUCE, a sort of East Village comic portrait of a marriage stuck in hell.

Among other things, I seem to enjoy hearing (and making) the same joke over and over, something that Shawn and I both seem to have our characters do (sometimes to other people's irritation).

A lot of the humor in Shawn's AUNT DAN is how incredibly verbose Aunt Dan is, that she just about buries you with her words. I found her intriguing and funny.

Then there's a section of Shawn's play — which I make reference to in my parody — in which Aunt Dan graduates from praising Kissinger's war policies to praising Hitler's extermination of the Jews. She isn't exactly in favor of it, but she nonetheless finds it "refreshing," she says, that the Nazis would act on their beliefs that the Jews were ruining their society, just as if you had cockroaches in your apartment, you, of course, would want to get rid of them.

Shawn's point in presenting this is to shock us with Aunt Dan's barbaric opinions, but he does this scary thing: he puts no one in the play to rebut her, he just makes the audience sit there, listening to this highly inflammatory, upsetting rhetoric.

So I liked the play. But it's a difficult one for some audiences to take.

Then, a year or so later, I saw a production of Giradoux's charming fable THE MADWOMAN OF CHAILLOT; and seeing it again, I have to admit that I was a bit taken aback by the ending: the charming Madwoman, the epitome of everything lovely and poetic and life-affirming, sends the wicked industrialists to their deaths because she realized they were ruining "her" Paris.

Now obviously in fable terms, the Madwoman's actions are meant to be embraced as the good person getting rid of the evil in the world. But I found that the Madwoman's certainty that she knew who was bad and who wasn't, and who should live and who shouldn't, made me suddenly uncomfortable. I started to find her not a little unlike Shawn's Aunt Dan. And unlike Aunt Dan, whom Shawn means us to squirm about, we're meant to find the Madwoman adorable.

So I wrote this parody.

CHARACTERS

THE MADWOMAN, a charming lady in a big hat
AUNT DAN, an intense, talkative intellectual

AUNT DAN MEETS THE MADWOMAN OF CHAILLOT

Scene: The Madwoman's bedroom in her cellar.

MADWOMAN.   Hello. As you may remember from last week, I just asked all the businessmen who are trying to ruin my beautiful world over here to my basement boudoir under the pretense of looking for oil, and then I shut them up in my sewer, where they all died horribly, I imagine. But the point is that the world is beautiful again, or, as we said before I was translated into English, *la monde est belle encore*. And now let's have tea.

How I love cinnamon tea. As I said to Gabrielle the other day, why did no one tell me the world had turned rotten, with industrialists and bankers and whatnot poisoning our world. I asked Madame Josephine if I was allowed to just kill them, and she said I was, if there was a trial, so before they got here, we gave them a trial and we found them guilty, and we simply locked them up in the sewer that so inexplicably is behind a door in my boudoir. Well, I'm madcap, I'll say that for me.

And now, because my usual friends are all in the hospital due to a car crash — Madame Constance insists on driving even though she's half blind and doesn't have a license, and we feel that the regulation of driving vehicles is just one other example of the state honing in on the freedom of the individual and on mankind's innate joie de vivre — in any case, they're all in the hospital with whiplash and broken bones and slipped disks — except for the ones in the other car who died, but we believe that the ones who died were rich industrialists so we feel it was all right — so with all these people in the hospital I've asked my good friend Aunt Dan to come to tea. *(Enter Aunt Dan.)* Hello, Aunt Dan. *(Holds up tea cup.)* Lemon?

AUNT DAN.   Thank you, I'll just have it plain with three heaping teaspoonfuls of sugar, I don't care what it does to my system, I just love the feeling. How marvelous to see you. Let me tell you what I think about Henry Kissinger. I think Kissinger is a genius. I mean the man is an utter genius. I mean when he looks at all the government briefings on his desk, and decides yes on one, and no on another, he is only committed to making our lives — the ones you and I live as Americans ...

MADWOMAN. *Je suis francaise.*

AUNT DAN. Right, you're a frog. Well, in any case, Kissinger looks around at the world and he says, by God, these people live a comfortable life, how can I best safeguard it for them? And does he say I can safeguard it by being nice? By being sweet? By looking at the North Vietnamese and saying, okay, we'll trust you because we believe it's polite to give you the benefit of a doubt? That's what namby pamby liberals might want him to do, but no, he takes it on his shoulder that in order for you and me to sit in this charming outside garden ...

MADWOMAN. This is a basement.

AUNT DAN. Don't interrupt me ... and have tea, it will be necessary for him to bomb the living daylights out of those North Vietnamese, and if some members of the liberal press don't like this, well, then, let them, because Henry Kissinger doesn't care about being liked, he cares about doing what is necessary to keep the world that you and I live in a comfortable place to live in. Think about cockroaches.

MADWOMAN. *(Alarmed.)* Do you see any?

AUNT DAN. Ssssh, don't interrupt me. The point is if you see a cockroach, you automatically want to kill it because it affects your way of life adversely. Oh, you might want to have tea and a piece of cake, say ...

MADWOMAN. Would you like a piece of cake?

AUNT DAN. I would love one, but please don't interrupt me. And you go to get this piece of cake, and there's this cockroach next to it.

MADWOMAN. Do you see a cockroach somewhere?

AUNT DAN. Aurelia, please, this is hypothetical. I neither know nor care whether you have cockroaches presently, I am trying to make a point about Henry Kissinger and the North Vietnamese. Now say you have this cockroach next to your nice piece of cake ...

MADWOMAN. *(Picking up the cake.)* I don't see one.

AUNT DAN. ... so you say, quite logically, well, I don't want it here, it affects my way of life, I want it killed. And so you kill it. And so that's what Henry Kissinger does for us. He bombs the North Vietnamese so you and I can have our tea.

MADWOMAN. Heavens, I don't want him to do that. I won't have tea if he kills people. I can have lemonade.

AUNT DAN. But don't you see, whether you have tea or lemonade or carbonated water with orange slices, Henry Kissinger is going to have to bomb a country. He can't not do it, because although it wouldn't interfere with your having tea today or tomorrow, it might eventually. How would you like it if you were having tea or playing cards or playing *dominoes,* and in walked the North Vietnamese, and they set your bed on fire, and made you become a communist, and dressed you in regulation rice paddy clothes, and there was no Henry Kissinger to protect you. At that point, just because you were squeamish about letting Kissinger go about and do his business early on, now it would be up to *you* to kill them. How would you handle that?

MADWOMAN. Well, I was going to tell you if you'd ever take a breath for a moment, that I just finished killing some people a few moments before you came. I lured some industrialists down here, and sent them through that door into the sewer, and locked the door, and now the world is beautiful again. *Et maintenant la monde est belle encore.*

AUNT DAN. I say this is rather exciting. I didn't know you killed people. I had this most exciting friend who was a trollop and a tramp and had sex in the most varied and disgusting combinations and she used to kill people for money or just for the thrill of it, and I thought she was super. And here I thought you were just this dopey woman with a lot of feathers in your head. Well, I say, that's just fantastic. Maybe you and I and Henry Kissinger could have sex together one day, and then kill someone.

MADWOMAN. Good heavens, I fear you have misunderstood my motives. Goodness, I don't think I want to have tea with you at all. *(Takes tea cup back.)* I believe in romance. I don't have sex with people. I had a romance with Adolphe Bertaut twenty years ago, and every day I cry a little tear over that lost romance, but I don't really like to have anything to do with physical relations. Goodness, I bet if Adolphe and I had ever had relations I should have thrown up. I am a romantic, not a sensualist.

AUNT DAN.   Adolphe Bertaut. Is he perhaps related to that other famous Adolphe?

MADWOMAN.   Adolphe Menjou?

AUNT DAN.   No, not Adolphe Menjou. Adolph the fearless, the man who had the courage of his convictions, that admirable sage and fuhrer, Adolph Hitler.

MADWOMAN.   Hitler? Good God, you like Hitler? Please, you mustn't say that, you'll have people walking out of the theatre.

AUNT DAN.   Now, now, don't close your mind to it so quickly. I admit some of what Hitler did probably wasn't very nice ...

MADWOMAN.   Probably? I think I'm going to get the check. Oh, waiter!

AUNT DAN.   ... and that he made some people suffer who maybe need not have suffered ...

MADWOMAN.   That's right, I'm not in a restaurant. Oh, the cafes and bistros of Paris, how I love them.

AUNT DAN.   Would you shut up, I'm making a point about Hitler.

MADWOMAN.   Good God, I'm so sorry I asked you here today.

AUNT DAN.   But look at it this way. You may not agree with every little thing Hitler did, but wasn't his behavior in some ways rather refreshing?

MADWOMAN.   Refreshing?

AUNT DAN.   Well, yes. He wanted to protect his way of life, so that it was comfortable. Now he saw the Jews as what was wrong about his society. Now we may think he was wrong about that ...

MADWOMAN.   I should say so. My seamstress is Jewish, and I don't know what I would do without her.

AUNT DAN.   That's not the point. The point is that Hitler

was refreshingly honest about what to do about the problem. I mean we kill cockroaches when they offend us, which I'm sure from the cockroaches' point of view is not very nice. But we have to protect our way of life.

MADWOMAN. How dare you compare Jews to cockroaches? That is totally shocking.

AUNT DAN. All right, I apologize. It's not me speaking, it's Henry Kissinger. Besides, it's not saying Hitler was right to kill the Jews, it's just saying that isn't his honesty in doing what he felt he had to do refreshing and charming, and is it so different from things we do?

MADWOMAN. It's very different from things I do.

AUNT DAN. You just shut up eight or twelve industrialists in your sewer. I hardly think that is so far above what Hitler did in theory, only in numbers.

MADWOMAN. How terribly ignorant you are, Aunt Dan. Hitler killed people who didn't deserve to die. I killed people who I felt had to be exterminated in order that Paris could blossom in the spring again.

AUNT DAN. But it's the same thing, except that you're pretentious about it.

MADWOMAN. How dare you say I'm pretentious?

AUNT DAN. Well, you refuse to see my point that Hitler and Kissinger acted logically out of the beliefs they held. You are a pigheaded French pastry.

MADWOMAN. You know, Aunt Dan, I think I left my lorgnette back there in the darker recesses of this basement. Would you mind going there for me, to fetch them?

AUNT DAN. Into the darker recesses of the basement? Well, why don't you fetch your lorgnette yourself?

MADWOMAN. Why don't I fetch it myself? Well, something's wrong with my legs suddenly. Every so often I forget how to move them, and this is one of those "every so often" 's.

AUNT DAN. Well, all right, but then I think I may have to leave after that. I'm having tea with the Gotti crime family. I mean, I know they're Mafia, but they're so charmingly honest about what they do that I find it hard not to like them.

MADWOMAN. Yes, yes, you see charm in the most monstrous

places, I get it. Please, go get my lorgnette. It's somewhere over there, where it's dark. Hurry please, Aunt Dan.

AUNT DAN. Very well. *(Aunt Dan exits into darkness. From off-stage.)* Goodness, it's dark over here. I can't see anything. I don't know how I'll be able to find your lorgnette, I can't see where I'm walking.

MADWOMAN. *(Calling to her, cheerfully.)* Watch out for the open pit that leads to hell.

AUNT DAN. *(From offstage.)* What? *(Screams.)* AAAAAAAAAA-AAHHHHHHHHHHHHHH! *(Momentary silence.)*

MADWOMAN. *(Chuckles to herself.)* Oh, well. Really, Aunt Dan didn't deserve to live, any more than those industrialists who were ruining my beloved Paris. Oh, what a responsibility it is to know who's good and who's bad, and to have to kill people — not really kill, I'm not like Hitler or the Gotti family — I have a French accent, and everything I do is to safeguard art and beauty and Paris. Let me finish my tea. *(Madwoman goes to sip her tea.)* I hope Aunt Dan hasn't poisoned my tea at some point when I wasn't looking. *(Sips her tea; screams.)* Aaaaaaaaaaaaaaa-gggghhhhh! Oh, *merde!* Sorry, I shouldn't swear, even in French, but my tea is poison, I think I'm going to d(ie).... *(Madwoman slumps over dead. End.)*

PROPERTY LIST

Tea cup (MADWOMAN)
Piece of cake (MADWOMAN)

DESIRE, DESIRE, DESIRE

DESIRE, DESIRE, DESIRE was first presented as part of an evening called MRS. SORKEN PRESENTS at American Repertory Theatre (Robert Bruestein, Artistic Director; Robert J. Orchard) in Cambridge, Massachusetts. It was directed by R. J. Cutler and Wesley Savick; the set design was by Loy Arcenas; the costume design was by Karen Eister; the lighting design was by Frank Butler; and the sound was by Steven Santomenna. The cast was as follows:

BLANCHE...Sandra Shipley
STANLEY ....James Andreassi
YOUNG MAN...Samuel Sifton
MAGGIE; CORA ....Harriet Harris
BIG DADDY ....Thomas Derrah
MAGGIE 2 ....Pamela Gien
STELLA ....Nina Bernstein

Recently, this play was done again, as part of MIX AND MATCH DURANG, at the John Drew Theatre, in East Hampton, New York, in June 1997. Directed by Elizabeth Gottlieb, Claire Lautier was BLANCHE, Jonathan Walker was STANLEY, Michael Ian Black was the YOUNG MAN, Jennifer Van Dyck was MAGGIE, Penny Balfour was CORA, Peter Jacobson was BIG DADDY, Penny Balfour was MAGGIE 2, and Jennifer Van Dyck was STELLA.

CHARACTERS

BLANCHE, sensitive and on the brink
STANLEY, a sexy lout
YOUNG MAN, an 18-year-old census taker
MAGGIE, desperate and in her slip
CORA, a good-time gal
BIG DADDY, very fat and angry about mendacity
MAGGIE 2, also desperate and also in her slip
STELLA, Blanche's sister

NOTE: MAGGIE and CORA may be double-cast, as may MAGGIE 2 and STELLA, if you can do the costume change fast enough.

DESIRE, DESIRE, DESIRE

Scene: A shabby New Orleans apartment.

Stanley in a ripped T-shirt sits at the table, guzzling beer. Blanche, dressed in frilly feminine clothes that contrast with Stanley's slobbiness, is sipping a cocktail and trying to look elegant.

Stanley finishes his beer, crushes it on his head and throws it on the ground. Blanche winces slightly. Stanley opens another beer and downs half of it, pouring the rest of it over his T-shirt.

STANLEY. *(Sighing in satisfaction.)* Ahhhhhh!

BLANCHE. Yes, it is rather hot, isn't it? Humid weather always makes me feel nervous, the least little sound makes me jump. *(Silence. Suddenly Stanley lets out with an enormous yell. Blanche just about jumps out of her skin.)*

STANLEY. Stella!!!!!!!

BLANCHE. Good Lord, Stanley, you startled me half to death. Oh if I only I knew a doctor who could give me a sedative.

STANLEY. What's a sedative?

BLANCHE. Oh, you'll never need one, you great big lout.

STANLEY. I am not a Polack! I am an American!

BLANCHE. I didn't say you were a Polack, Stanley, I said you were a lout.

STANLEY. Oh, that's different. *(Suddenly bellowing again.)* STELLA!!!!

BLANCHE. Stanley, please, you must stop doing that. My nerves. Besides, Stella isn't coming back. She went out that door to get me a lemon Coke about six years ago, and the fact she hasn't returned leads me to believe she doesn't intend to.

STANLEY. Where'd my baby go? I miss her. STELLA!!!!

BLANCHE. Oh Lord. There's no hope. *(Doorbell.)* Oh good, the doorbell. *(Stanley burps. Blanche goes to the door, lets in a Young Man.)*

YOUNG MAN. Good evening, Ma'am. I'm the census taker.

BLANCHE. I see. How interesting. Won't you come in?

YOUNG MAN. Thank you, Ma'am.

BLANCHE. Look, Stanley, how nicely he's dressed. And his carriage shows off his figure. Yes, a woman can notice a young man's figure sometimes, when she's feeling desperate and wanting to escape from her dreadful life by indulging for a few moments, or a few hours, of ... desire.

STANLEY. What?

BLANCHE. Nothing, Stanley. Just talking to myself.

YOUNG MAN. How many people live here?

BLANCHE. Five. Stanley, myself, the milkman, the paper boy, and the French pastry chef.

STANLEY. French pastries are sissy.

BLANCHE. You're just not a *gourmet*, Stanley. We have to work on expanding your taste buds.

YOUNG MAN. And what are the professions of the people who live here?

BLANCHE. Well, the milkman is a milkman, the paper boy delivers paper, the pastry chef cooks pastry, Mr. Kowalski here drinks beer and bowls on Monday, and I create an atmosphere of elegance and refinement, and just a little bit of magic. Would you like to come in the other room and lie down with me?

YOUNG MAN. What?

BLANCHE. Oh, nothing, it's just you remind me of someone else, someone young and tender who touched my heart when I was a young girl at Belle Reeve. Oh, desire, desire, desire. Stanley, I'm hot. Cool me off. *(Stanley throws a can of beer in her face.)* Oh, thank you. Refreshing. Some people wash their hair in beer, did you know that? Stanley doesn't wash his hair though, do you, Stanley?

STANLEY. Lay off.

BLANCHE. And he doesn't use a deodorant. I really can't stand being here with him, if it weren't for the milkman, and the paper boy and the pastry chef, why, I do declare, I'd just go mad.

STANLEY. I bought you a bus ticket. Why don't you never use it?

194

BLANCHE. I'm waiting for Stella to come back, Stanley.

STANLEY. Stella!!!!

BLANCHE. Waiting, waiting. If only we knew.

YOUNG MAN. Are you registered Democrats or Republicans?

BLANCHE. Oh I'm sorry. I forgot you were here. Did anyone ever tell you look like a prince out of the Arabian nights? — 'cause you do, honey lamb.

STANLEY. What poetry.

BLANCHE. Mr. Kowalski doesn't like poetry. He rejects the elevated visions of Wordsworth, Sheets and Kelly. *(Correcting herself.)* Kates and Shelley. Keets and Shelley. And Gerald Manley Hophead. Hopscotch. Oh, I'm all confused.

YOUNG MAN. Are you registered Democrats or Republicans?

BLANCHE. I'm a registered southern belle. I belong to the party of the heart, but I have been foolish, I have cast my pearls to swine. Do you want to come in the other room and lie down for a while?

YOUNG MAN. What, Ma'am?

BLANCHE. Oh, nothing. Desire, desire, desire. Hit me again, Stanley. *(Stanley throws another beer in her face.)* Oh, thank you. Very refreshing. Mr. Kowalski does come in handy sometimes.

YOUNG MAN. When will the milkman and the paper boy and the pastry chef be back so I could ask them questions?

BLANCHE. You pose such difficult queries. How can I say when they will be back, or even if they're coming back? I'm such a needy person, I scare them all away. Are you sure you don't want to lie down in the other room for a while?

YOUNG MAN. Thank you kindly, Ma'am, but I'm on the job. *(Enter Maggie, in a white slip. She goes up to Stanley.)*

MAGGIE. *(To Stanley.)* Brick, Brick. Big Daddy is dying of cancer and he wants us to have a child, Brick. And you can't want Gooper and Mae and the no-neck monsters to inherit all the money, do you, Brick?

BLANCHE. Do you have the right apartment?

MAGGIE. *(Looks around, sees she's in the wrong place.)* Oh, I'm sorry. *(To Stanley, friendly.)* Good-bye. *(Exits.)*

BLANCHE. Young, young, young man.

YOUNG MAN. Yes?

BLANCHE. Wait, I've forgotten what I was going to say. *(Thinks.)* Oh yes. Don't you just love these long rainy afternoons in New Orleans when an hour isn't just an hour — but a little drop of eternity dropped into your hands?

YOUNG MAN. Not really.

BLANCHE. Well, fuck you.

STANLEY. That's tellin' him.

BLANCHE. *(Deeply apologetic.)* Oh, I'm sorry. How rude of me. I'm just half-mad with desire. I feel like a cat on a hot tin roof. *(Reenter Maggie.)*

MAGGIE. Brick, Brick, I know about you and Skipper. You disgust me.

BLANCHE. You have the wrong apartment, go away!

MAGGIE. *(Looks at them; realizes again.)* Oh, I *beg* your pardon. I have dyslexia and I must be reading the number on your door backwards. I have to remember to reverse everything I see, and I get all confused. You should see me dial a phone. It's hilarious. *(Pause.)* Good-bye! *(Exits.)*

STANLEY. I used to have a cousin who could open a beer bottle with his teeth. And then when snap-top cans became popular, he became all ashamed and useless. He became a geek in a carnival and now he bites the heads off of chickens they sell in the supermarket before they wrap them in cellophane and put them in the meat counter.

BLANCHE. Thank you for sharing that, Stanley. It was fascinating. *(To Young Man.)* He talks so rarely, I think it's important to encourage him when he does.

YOUNG MAN. Are you in favor of tuition tax credits for citizens who send their children to private school?

BLANCHE. Oh I don't know. Ask me something about art, or poetry.

YOUNG MAN. Do you think "Ode on a Grecian Urn" is John Keats' best poem?

STANLEY. What's a Grecian urn?

BLANCHE. Oh, about 3.50 an hour. *(Laughs hysterically.)* Oh, my God, I've made a joke, I'm so sorry. *(Enter Cora, dressed in a bright polka-dot, trampy-dress. She has a corny New York accent, saying "Poil" for "Pearl" and "goil" for "girl." Etc.)*

196

CORA.   Hiya, everybody. Beejees, me and Pearl was just at Harry Hope's saloon talkin' about pipe dreams, and Hickey came in for his usual bender, and he told his iceman story that he tells every year, and then he said we all had too many pipe dreams, and when Chuck and me talked about our pipe dream of savin' up enough money to get married and live on a farm if only Chuck could stay on the wagon for a coupla weeks, Hickey looked at us with this kinda mean smile on his ugly map, and he said, beejees, *pipe dreams*, you kids run your life wid *pipe dreams*, but I just killed my wife and now I know I don't got no *pipe dreams*, and, Pearl, you'd be better off without *pipe dreams* too, and so Chuck and me realize we did have a *pipe dream* our lives would get better, but now we see that ain't gonna happen, I'm a whore and he's a drunk. But at least we ain't got no *pipe dreams* anymore!

BLANCHE.   *(Irritated.)* Please, please! You've said the word "pipe dream" fifty times! Can't you say the word "illusion?" "Illusion," "illusion." Try it.

CORA.   So we've given up our ... *(Says it slowly.)* ... il-lu-sions ... and we want everyone else to too. *(Energetically to Blanche.)* Face it, you're old and ugly, you're never going to find happiness, and you're going to end up in a mental institution. There! Don't that make you feel better?

BLANCHE.   *(Trying to give the concept the benefit of the doubt.)* I don't ... think so. Let me just go throw up in the other room, and then I'll tell you. *(Runs out.)*

CORA.   Did I upset her? Beejees, I didn't mean to upset her. Chuck and me, we wuz cheered up when we let go of our pipe dreams ... il-lu-sions.

STANLEY.   Oh, Blanche is so sensitive it makes you wanna barf. *(Towards the bathroom.)* Hey, canary bird, get outta the bathroom, I gotta pee! *(Reenter Blanche.)*

BLANCHE.   No need to shout, Stanley. Young man, you are going to have to change the information on your census sheet. There will be only four people living here in a few minutes.

STANLEY.   You're finally going to use the bus ticket. Hot damn.

BLANCHE.   No, Stanley. I am making an exit, but it's going to be a final one, Stanley. Because it's so long, Sam; it's good-bye, Charlie; it's 'night, mother. *(Takes out long sheet of paper.)* Now I've made a list of where everything is so you won't be confused. The paper lanterns are in the top shelf in the bed-room closet, along with broken dreams and extra filters for the vacuum cleaner. The little white tie-things that go with the plastic garbage bags are up above the refrigerator in an empty Nestles Quick box. Extra ice trays are under the bed along with the papers about Belle Reeve and old love letters, yellowin' with antiquity. But you're not to read the love letters, I want to be buried with them.

STANLEY. Yeah, yeah, yeah.

BLANCHE.   There are sour balls and Hostess Twinkies in the second cabinet next to the refrigerator, and there are Hershey bars and peanut brittle in the third draw in the kitchen next to the fire extinguisher and the Aunt Jemima cookie jar. The Eiffel Tower place settings are in the fourth drawer along with the orange juice squeezer and the paper napkins, and scattered pieces of my heart. Linen napkins are in the hall closet with the towels and licorice strings, but I don't want you usin' the linen towels, Stanley Kowalski, I want to be buried with them too.

STANLEY.   *(Not able to remember.)* Where's the peanut brittle?

BLANCHE.   In the third drawer in the kitchen, next to the fire extinguisher.

STANLEY.   I might get some later.

CORA.   Me too.

BLANCHE.   Isn't anyone going to try to talk me out of suicide?

CORA.   *(Friendly but a bit off-hand.)* Oh, sure, honey. Don't go kill yourself.

BLANCHE.   No, I must.

CORA.   How come you wanna kill yourself?

BLANCHE.   Young woman, I'm at the end of my rope.

CORA.   Don't use a rope. Use the bus ticket Stanley gave you.

BLANCHE.   It's a ticket to somewhere called Glengarry Glen Ross, and I don't want to go there.

STANLEY.   *(Suddenly very energetic, staccato, aggressive.)* Why the fuck not? The place is good. It's not great maybe, but what I'm sayin' is, it's good. Not great, good. That's what I'm sayin'. It may be swamp, it may have bugs, but fuck, Blanche, what's perfect? You tell me. No, don't tell me, I'll tell you. It's not great, good. Am I right? Do you understand what I'm sayin'? Should I say it again? What I'm sayin' is, fuck shit piss damn, it ain't half bad. Half good, half bad. You gotta settle. It ain't perfect. Settle. Gotta. You gotta settle. A negotiation. Give and take. You know what I'm sayin'? What I'm sayin' is ...

BLANCHE. Shut up. I know what you're saying. She says pipe dream 300 times, you repeat yourself endlessly. It's life-like, granted, one *could* hear it on a bus, if you were listening to a stupid person talking on and on, but I'm on a streetcar, not a bus, and I want poetry and art and music, and if I can't have them, I'd rather be dead.

STANLEY. What I'm sayin' is you gotta be fuckin' realistic.

BLANCHE. I don't want realism, I want magic!

YOUNG MAN. Well, I've been silent for a very long time.

BLANCHE. Yes, and I've appreciated it. Thank you.

YOUNG MAN. But now I want to talk about cable TV.

BLANCHE. What?

YOUNG MAN. There's constant need for new product. This is my last week as a census taker. Next week I'm starting my new job as vice-president in charge of script development for Home Box Office. We're always on the look-out for new ideas. Comedies about attractive people who have terminal cancer. Dramas about handicapped people who learn to run in the Olympics with a wooden leg. Musicals about high school students with bubonic plague who raise money to send homeless people to dancing school. Laughter, tears, exploitation. So if any of you have any ideas, here's my card.

BLANCHE. Thank you, honey lamb.

CORA. Excuse me, I'm going to go get some peanut brittle. *(Exits.)*

BLANCHE. Young man, why don't you make a program about me? A woman with illusions shattered, livin' in a place where death is as close as you are, and where the opposite of death is desire. Desire, desire, desire.

199

YOUNG MAN.   I don't mean to be rude, but I don't think you're commercial enough. *(Enter Big Daddy, looking enormously fat and round, with fat padding that makes him look like Tweedledee and Tweedledum. He has a big cigar in his mouth.)*

BIG DADDY.   Brick, Brick. Big Mama is drivin' me crazy, Mae and Gooper are drivin' me crazy, why can't you and Maggie the Cat have a child together? What's the matter between you and Maggie, Brick? *(Enter Maggie, but played by a different actress than who played it before. She is Maggie 2, and is wearing the same slip as the first one. She crosses to Stanley.)*

MAGGIE 2.   Brick, you left your crutches in the other room, Brick. It's my time of month to conceive now, Brick. Do you want to go in the other room and lie down?

BLANCHE.   That sounds like me. *(To Young Man.)* You don't want to go lie down, do you, desire desire? *(Young Man politely shakes his head "no.")*

MAGGIE 2.   Brick, what's the matter between us? *(The first Maggie comes in from the kitchen, from where Cora had exited. She is the first Maggie, and she is chomping on a piece of peanut brittle.)*

MAGGIE.   Brick, honey, you want some peanut brittle? It's good, baby. *(Maggie 1 and Maggie 2 look at one another, both feeling threatened.)*

BIG DADDY.   I'd like some peanut brittle. *(Exits to the kitchen.)*

MAGGIE 2.   Brick, I want to have your baby.

MAGGIE.   *I* want to have his baby.

STANLEY.   Stella!!!!!

BLANCHE.   Please, there seems to be some misunderstanding. Can't the two of you go away and sort it out? I feel as if I'm not at the center of attention when you're both here, and it distresses me.

MAGGIE 2.   *(To Stanley.)* Is it because of Skipper that you won't go to bed with me? *(She goes over to the Young Man, addresses him as Skipper.)* Skipper, is that the reason?

BIG DADDY.   *(Entering from kitchen, eating peanut brittle.)* Mendacity, mendacity! *(Exits back to kitchen.)*

MAGGIE 2.   Brick, Brick, I'll tell you where I'm hiding the alcohol if you'll go to bed with me.

MAGGIE.   Will you leave him alone?

200

MAGGIE 2. I feel like a cat on a hot tin roof.

MAGGIE. *I* feel like a cat on a hot tin roof.

BLANCHE. I feel left out. Please, everyone leave, this is my apartment, and my story, and my sensitivity, and my desire, so I want you all outta here. Except for Stanley.

STANLEY. SKIPPER!!!!! *(Puts his arm around the Young Man's shoulder.)* Maggie the cat, you make everything dirty. What's between me is Skipper is good and holy and there ain't nothing dirty about. Oh, sometimes when we wuz on the road together, we'd reach across the bed and shake hands, like men would. Oh, and sometimes, if it was hot, we might take showers together. And sometimes, if we had nothin' better to do, we might dress up like lumberjacks and French kiss for an hour, but it was nothin' dirty. Was it, Skipper?

YOUNG MAN. I don't quite know what to say.

STANLEY. Skipper!!!!

YOUNG MAN. *(Agreeably, conversationally.)* Brick.

MAGGIE 2. *(Desperate.)* Brick!

MAGGIE. *(Desperate.)* Brick!

BIG DADDY. *(Entering from the kitchen.)* Big Mama! Big Mama! Oooooohhh! *(Exits.)*

STANLEY. *(To Young Man.)* Come on, Skipper, you and me is gonna go back to high school together, and play on the football team again. And go find a motel room. Don't that sound great?

YOUNG MAN. I'm sorry. What? *(Stanley and Young Man exit.)*

MAGGIE 2. Brick!

MAGGIE. Brick! *(The two Maggie's exit. Big Daddy comes in from the kitchen, carrying lots of bags of candy and various things mentioned in Blanche's suicide speech.)*

BIG DADDY. Thank you for your kind hospitality, Ma'am. *(Exits. Blanche is still for a moment or two.)*

BLANCHE. *(Suddenly.)* Oh my God, I'm alone! *(Runs to door.)* Help! Help! I'm all alone! Help! Help! *(Runs to where the kitchen is.)* Help! Help! I'm alone! *(Goes to telephone.)* Operator, operator, get me Western Union, I want to send a telegram! "Help, help, caught in a trap, can't stand solitude, am afraid I'll go mad. Signed Blanche DuBois." What? Beckett? Samuel Beckett? No, I don't know him. Uh-huh. Uh-huh. I see. All right. *(Hangs up; sits, stares out; lights dim to a spotlight on her.)* Nothing to be done. We'll just keep waiting. Waiting for Stella to come back with the lemon Coke. Year after year, staring ahead with our lips tightly compressed. Waiting, waiting. *(Lights start to dim, as if play is over. But then they come back up to pretty full, somewhat to Blanche's surprise as well. Stella then enters. She carries a large paper cup of Coca-Cola.)*

STELLA. Blanche, honey, I'm back with your lemon Coke. *(Blanche looks pretty surprised to see her.)* I'm sorry I was gone so many years. The store on the corner was closed. Where's Stanley?

BLANCHE. He went off to a motel with a young man, rather like my first husband did. We have trouble choosing men, Stella.

STELLA. Oh, Stanley, he's such a card. Well, are you happy to see your baby sister, Blanche?

BLANCHE. Stella, Stella for star. At last my lemon Coke. My nerves have needed a lemon Coke. *(Goes to sip the Coca-Cola.)* Stella for Star. This is not a lemon Coke. This is a cherry Coke. *(Hands the Coca-Cola back.)*

STELLA. Oh, I'm sorry.

BLANCHE. Would you mind bringin' it back and gettin' the proper one for me? My nerves need a lemon Coke, honey.

STELLA. Sure, Blanche. I'll be back as soon as I can. *(Exits with the Coke.)*

BLANCHE. *(Said fairly quickly; not fast exactly, but each thought should "feed" into the next.)* She's gone. I'm all alone. For six more years at least. Alone, alone. All alone. Oh desire, desire, desire. Desire under the elms; desire under the arms. Farewell to arms. For whom the bell tolls. For whom the *southern* belle tolls. Waiting, waiting. Nothing to be done. We stare out, our lips compressed. Christ on the cross. One of the thieves was saved. One of the thieves had roast beef. One of the thieves went wee wee wee, all the way home. You can never go home again, Blanche. I, I, I took the blows in my face and my body. Body, body. Is anybody there? Stanley? Stella? Young, young, young man? One of the Maggies? Oh please, God, let someone come to the door. *(She runs to the door, opens it. It is a man in a very large rabbit suit.)*

RABBIT.   *Flores. Flores para los muertos.*

BLANCHE.   Are you, Harvey? From the Pulitzer prize-winning play by Mary Chase? That was a lean year. *(Rabbit shakes head "no.")* You're not Harvey. Well, whoever you are, I have always depended on the kindness of strangers. *(The Rabbit takes off its head, revealing Stanley.)* Stanley. You're back. What about Skipper.

STANLEY.   It was a phase. It's over now.

BLANCHE.   Why are you wearing the rabbit suit, Stanley?

STANLEY.   I wore this rabbit suit on my wedding night, and I'm gonna wear it again when Stella has a baby, and then I'm gonna rip it off and wave it like a flag.

BLANCHE.   Is Stella pregnant, Stanley?

STANLEY.   I don't know. I ain't seen her in six years.

BLANCHE.   *(Remembering.)* Oh, she was back briefly while you were out with Skipper and all those Maggies. But she went off again.

STANLEY.   She was here? And she left? When's my baby comin' back, Blanche? When's she comin' back?

BLANCHE.   I don't know, Stanley. I don't know. Well, Stanley, it's you and me again.

STANLEY.   We've had this date from the beginning.

BLANCHE.   Yes, we have. Sweet of you to say so.

STANLEY.   Stella!!!!

BLANCHE.   Oh, you're back on that again.

STANLEY.   Stella!!!!

BLANCHE.   Oh God, there's no hope. *(Sits.)*

STANLEY.   Stella!!!!!

BLANCHE.   Oh desire, desire, desire.

STANLEY.   Stella!!!!! *(Mournful saxophone music. Blanche sadly puts the rabbit head on her own head. She sits there, tragically, sadly. Lights dim. End.)*

PROPERTY LIST

Cans of beer (STANLEY)
Large cocktail (BLANCHE)
Long sheet of paper (BLANCHE)
Cigar (BIG DADDY)
Peanut Brittle (MAGGIE, BIG DADDY)
Bags of candy (BIG DADDY)
Bags of household items (BIG DADDY)
Paper cup of Coca-Cola (STELLA)

AUTHOR'S NOTE

Afterword

DESIRE, DESIRE, DESIRE is a parody of several Tennessee Williams' plays.

The play premiered at A.R.T. Recently it was presented as part of an evening in East Hampton. I think one has to especially look at the part of Blanche, and make sure that even though she has a Southern accent and is romantic that she keeps a sense of pace about her. She rarely has an action, she's all talk ... and so it falls to the director and actress to make the audience feel as if the play is moving ahead. Also, be careful of long vowels in the Southern accent. They're accurate, but they slow the rhythms down. Find some happy medium, find a way to have a Southern accent but still go fast in some of the speeches.

Some additional things:

Most people who know theatre well will get the allusions I'm making in this play, but in case there are some readers who aren't certain, I'm going to risk being obvious and just out and out tell you who's from what.

Blanche, Stanley, Stella and the Young Man are from Williams' A STREETCAR NAMED DESIRE.

Big Daddy and Maggie are from Williams' CAT ON A HOT TIN ROOF.

Cora is a character from O'Neill's THE ICEMAN COMETH.

When Blanche gives a long list of "where everything is," for Stanley to know after she's dead, this is a reference to and parody of Marsha Norman's play 'NIGHT, MOTHER.

When Stanley does his "why the fuck not" speech, it's an allusion to David Mamet's GLENGARRY GLEN ROSS. (NOTE: This Mamet parody speech is the same one that appears in STYE OF THE EYE.)

And the man in the rabbit suit, as is mentioned in the play, is a reference to Mary Chase's popular comedy from the late 1940s, HARVEY, where James Stewart played a chatty man who drove his sister crazy by talking to his invisible friend, Harvey the rabbit.

CARDINAL O'CONNOR

CARDINAL O'CONNOR was included in URBAN BLIGHT, an evening of sketches by twenty authors, which premiered May 18, 1988, at the Manhattan Theatre Club, in New York City.

CARDINAL O'CONNOR ....Rex Robbins

Subsequently, this sketch was part of A MESS OF PLAYS BY CHRIS DURANG in 1996 at South Coast Repertory, in Costa Mesa, California, with Hal Landon, Jr. as CARDINAL O'CON-NOR.

CARDINAL O'CONNOR

VOICE. And now, Cardinal John O'Connor will speak to you about the condom. *(Enter Cardinal O'Connor dressed in red clerical robes; he is bouncing a basketball as he comes out as well, and is wearing sneakers.)*

CARDINAL O'CONNOR. Hi, there. I was just playing basketball with Mayor Ed Koch. Got a lot of baskets, didn't have time to change my sweatsocks. Hope I don't smell.

Anyway, I'm glad to be here today to talk to you about the condom.

Now it was reported in the New York *Times* that the National Bishops Committee, of which I am a member, just put out a statement about AIDS saying that even though contraception is objectively, morally wrong, that because not everyone else follows this Catholic belief, it might be acceptable to educate people that the condom can in some ways protect you from AIDS, as long as it was stressed that abstinence was the only 100 percent safe way, and as long as it was also stressed that contraception and condoms are wrong. So that's what the report said.

Well, this Bishops report is not acceptable to me.

You can never justify a lesser evil by saying it prevents a larger evil. Now to put a condom on your penis is simply morally repugnant to God — as we in the Catholic Church have told you for centuries, although Christ never talked about condoms, he made the Catholic Church His spokesman, and we have explained until we're blue in the face that sex is for procreation, and that anything that interferes with procreation is wrong, it's wrong, it's wrong, it's wrong. Putting a condom on your penis is wrong.

I am a man of God, and I must point out to you what is wrong when it's wrong.

I don't care if it's not practical; I don't care if drug addicts and teenagers and homosexuals will run around giving each other AIDS and die — *(Catches how this sounds; adds deep compassion to his voice.)* well, that is, I do care, I care deeply about their suffering — *(His energy returns; firm:)* but we can only tell them to use abstinence: to never have sex again for the rest of their lives.

That is the only morally acceptable advice I can give them.

I am unwilling to have any teenagers or drug addicts or promiscuous girls or homosexuals hear anything else.

I have never had sex in my entire life, and I'm healthy and normal; so I do not ask anyone to do anything that I myself would not be able to do, and have not done.

Let's start abstinence clubs around the country. It can be fun.

One other thing — people have said to me, you were an army chaplain, you supported the Vietnam war, you allowed men the lesser evil of killing one another to stop the greater evil of communism.

How can you be such a stickler and say that the lesser evil of condom use is somehow not balanced by its stopping the greater evil of spreading AIDS and causing great suffering and death?

And futhermore, Christ and the Bible say "Thou shalt not kill" repeatedly throughout the Bible, and nowhere does anyone in the bible say, "Do not put a little plastic balloon on your penis."

Well, I have a good answer to the people who say that. Here is my answer. My answer is about to follow. Here it comes.

Killing people for a good cause is not evil.

Putting a balloon on your penis, for whatever reason, is always, always evil.

I hope I have cleared up any misconceptions you may have had. And so, until the next moral crisis comes along and I need to tell you what's moral and what isn't, so long! *(Goes out cheerfully, bouncing his basketball.)*

PROPERTY LIST

Basketball

AUTHOR'S NOTE

Afterword

CARDINAL O'CONNOR was written for a 1988 musical revue called URBAN BLIGHT that was produced by the Manhattan Theatre Club.

The theme of the evening, as implied by the title, was city life, especially in New York. So many of the sketches were about how hard it was to be alive in the city.

I think the CARDINAL O'CONNOR piece is self-explanatory. Cardinal O'Connor is the very public, very conservative Catholic cardinal in New York City, and he was particularly close to Mayor Ed Koch (they wrote a book together called HIS EMINENCE AND HIZZONER).

The Cardinal has been a big foe of sex education in high schools (or actually anywhere), and not just in Catholic schools. He wants everyone told to be abstinent, and wants that to be the total extent of the discussion.

In the age of AIDS, where condom use offers protection from the HIV virus, it seems actually criminal to work against getting that message out to the teens (and others) who are sexually active — especially when he is trying to impact *public* schools over which he has no jurisdiction. Practicality makes no dint in his feelings; when told many teenagers are already sexually active, his response is that they shouldn't be; and that telling them how to protect themselves encourages them to have sex (which they're already having, but no matter) and this he won't do and wants to stop anyone else from doing. So his idea is to tell all teenagers not to have sex, and to keep them in the dark about condom use that can (much of the time) protect them from AIDS.

And then he uses his political clout and tries to convince city government to do it his way. And why? Well his justification is the age old Catholic "sex-must-always-be-open-to-procreation" argument that seems to me juvenile and shoddy as logic. I believe the Cardinal is sincere; but I also believe he has done harm. So that is my topic.

The specific Bishop's report was current at the time of the sketch — 1988 — and the Cardinal did indeed feel it necessary to distance himself from the slight, slight liberal tone this Bishops' report took.

My fondest memory of the sketch at Manhattan Theatre Club was listening to a large audience of older New Yorkers react when the Cardinal had the line "we can only tell them to use abstinence: to never have sex again for the rest of their lives." The extremity of how that sounded "landed" one night, and the audience laughed and laughed and laughed at how far out this opinion was. And yet that *is* the Cardinal's and the Catholic Church's position offered to unmarried people and to gay people: never have sex ever, unless you marry. Forever.

To read the words of Christ in the gospels, where sex is rarely a topic, and then to juxtapose the centuries of obsessive, repressive teaching the Catholic Church has done on sexuality makes one want to laugh, or cry, or hit someone — in my case, all three.

THE BOOK OF
LEVITICUS SHOW

THE BOOK OF LEVITICUS SHOW was filmed on video in the "public access"-style for DURANG/DURANG at Manhattan Theatre Club, in New York City, in 1994. It was included in the first preview, and then cut from the evening due to length. It had the following cast:

LETTIE LU	Becky Ann Baker
TOMMY, HER HUSBAND (off-camera)	Marcus Giamatti
GRANDMA	Patricia Elliott
MAGGIE WILKINSON	Lizbeth Mackay
MAGGIE'S DAUGHTER	Keith Reddin
TWO GUESTS	David Aaron Baker, Patricia Randell

NOTE: The above cast list reflects the number of characters used in the video version filmed by director Walter Bobbie for the Manhattan Theatre Club evening.

The script I have prepared is written so it can be done on-stage, rather than on video. (Doing it on video lets you capture the look of public access TV; but stage is probably easier.)

In the stage version, the characters of motel owner Maggie Wilkinson and her daughter do *not* appear.

CHARACTERS

LETTIE LU
TOMMY, her husband and camera man
GRANDMA, Lettie Lu's mother
TWO GUESTS ON HER SHOW, a man and a woman

THE BOOK OF
LEVITICUS SHOW

Optional Introduction

VOICE.   You are watching the Wheeling, West Virginia Community Public Access Station, Channel 61. The West Virginia Community Public Access Station is in no way responsible for the content of any program on this channel. The views expressed belong to the public access individual producers. By law we must broadcast whatever people want to say. If we could shut down this entire public access station, we would be glad to. But by law we can't. So stay tuned for our next public access program, on Channel 61. We think it is a premiere episode.

Scene: A somewhat rundown motel room in West Virginia. A bed with an elderly Grandma asleep on it. An empty bird cage. Suitcases around, opened, not quite unpacked. A standing screen, with clothes flung up over the top. A chair. Near the chair is Lettie Lu, about 35, in a print dress, wandering around. She has a fair amount of energy. Her husband Tommy has a video camera, which he has trained on her. Tommy may best be out in the house, or at the back of the theatre.

LETTIE LU.   Are we on the air? *(Lettie Lu realizes that she is on the air, and talks out toward Tommy's camera. Sometimes she sits in her chair, sometimes she bounds up out of it, down to the edge of the stage, to be closer to the camera.)* Hello there. Can you hear me? If you can't hear me, call 556-7421, and ask for Lettie Lu in Room 12, and then I'll talk up. This here is our first show, and so I don't know if I need to shout.
TOMMY.   *(From behind the camera.)* You don't have to shout, Lettie.
LETTIE LU.   That's my husband Tommy. He's the cameraman. And this is Momma. Show Momma, Tommy. Momma is

eighty-three years old and she brought me up all her life in West Virginia and she's a good woman. Bring the camera back to me, Tommy, people must be tired of looking at Momma. *(Smiles at camera.)* Hi again. I'm Lettie Lu and this is the first BOOK OF LEVITICUS SHOW installment. *(Lettie Lu holds up a cardboard sign with the hand-painted words, "BOOK OF LEVITICUS SHOW.")*

Now I was minding my business back in Tommy's and my house in West Virginia. The children had growed up, one of them is a country Western star, one of them is a teller in a bank. Jimmy, he hasn't found himself yet, he don't do nothing. But we were havin' our quiet life when God set our house on fire. Well it wasn't God really, it was Momma; leastwise, we think it was Momma, she denies it, but who else was up cookin' at two in the morning, not me or Tommy, we wuz asleep.

But our house burned to the ground, all of it; and we wuz real bitter. We slept in the truck for a couple of nights, but then I said to Tommy, "What are we complainin' about, we got our lives. God gave us our lives, and we have got to be grateful."

And then we took the Bible out of the glove compartment, and I said, "Tommy, this is God's word, and it will comfort us." *(She picks up the Bible and shows us.)*

You know, you can open up the Bible to any old page and it will have a message for you. *(Chooses a section at random.)*

Like here, in the Book of Numbers: *(She reads:)*

"And the names of the men are these: of the tribes of Judah, Caleb the son of Jephunneh. And of the tribe of the children of Simeon, Shemeul, the son of Annihud. And the prince of the tribe of the children of Dan, Buddi the son of Jogli." Well this here don't mean a thing to us, but then we read that lovely passage about the Lord is thy shepherd and the green pastures, didn't we, Tommy?

TOMMY.   Yes, we sure did, Lettie.

LETTIE LU.   And we had some money in the bank, so we thought we'd just come on over to this motel, where the owner is a good Christian woman and her daughter with the harelip, but really it doesn't look bad if you don't look at it. And then

Tommy said, "Lettie, read another passage from the Bible."

And then I turned to the Book of Leviticus. *(Reads with great importance:)*

"And the man that committeth adultery with another man's wife, even he that committeth adultery with his neighbor's wife, the adulterer and the adulteress shall surely be put to death." *(Bounces out of her chair to explain this.)*

Well, that made a lot of sense to us because in all our years of marriage, and I married Tommy when I was fourteen or something just like Loretta Lynn did 'ceptin' I don't sing none; well, in all that time, Tommy and I has never been unfaithful to one another because we believe in God and religion and marriage. And I got to thinkin' about how people say they believe in the Bible but they don't follow through and do nothin' about it.

TOMMY. Sit back down and read them the other part, Lettie. *(Lettie Lu sits back down.)*

LETTIE LU. Oh yeah. This is from the same page as the thing about adultery. *(Reads from the Bible again:)*

"And if a man also lie with mankind, as he lieth with a woman, both of them have committed an abomination, they shall surely be put to death." *(Slams the Bible shut, bounces up again.)* Well, we checked with the minister about the wordin' just to make sure we understood, but what we thought was true *was* true: this is about homos! And notice that God says *surely* someone will put them to death. I mean, God thinks it's so much what the right thing to do, that he just *presumes* somebody's gonna do it for him!

But we've gotten mighty far from followin' God's commands.

TOMMY. Sit back down and get to the point, Lettie.

LETTIE LU. You're right, Tommy. So what we done is, we went to Sally Bowden's house, and she's got herself two strappin' big sons, Big Jake and Big Harry, and we went into town and Big Jake and Big Harry went out and they captured an adulteress and a homo for us, and they tied 'em up and brung 'em here. I mean, they're here right now. *(Lettie Lu goes and moves the screen. Behind it, tied up on the floor and with gags in their mouths, are a Woman and a Man. They struggle slightly; they've prob-ably been there a while.)* See? I kept 'em behind the screen to add to the suspense. I hope you like our show. It's our first episode.

TOMMY.   Get back to the point, Lettie.

LETTIE LU.   Oh right. And so now we're going to follow the teachings of God in the Book of Leviticus. Wake up, Momma. *(Lettie Lu goes over to Grandma, tries to wake her, but she seems to be sleeping deeply. To Grandma.)* We're gonna do the first ones. Momma. God, I hope she's not dead. Oh, there she goes. You havin' a dream, Momma?

GRANDMA.   Where's my teeth?

LETTIE LU.   Well, did you go to sleep with them in your mouth, or did you take them out first?

GRANDMA.   I don't know where they are.

LETTIE LU.   We know that, Momma. That wasn't the ques-tion. Now we are on television, and nobody out there wants to hear about your teeth.

GRANDMA.   I had a dream about pancakes.

LETTIE LU.   Pancakes? Oh dry up, Momma, you're irritatin' everybody. *(Gets a gun from somewhere easy.)*

Old age is a terrible thing. Okay, you ready, Tommy? *(Lettie Lu gets in a position, aims at the two people on the floor. Aims well, but maybe looks the other way; she's not blood-thirsty, just doing her best to follow the Bible.)*

Pay attention now, Momma, we're gonna kill 'em. In the name of God's will, you shall *surely* be put to death. *(Lettie Lu fires the gun twice. One or both of the bodies twitch violently; because they're tied together, it's hard to tell if one or both has been hit.)*

Did I get 'em, Tommy?

TOMMY.   Looks like it. Wrap it up now, Lettie, we're outta time.

GRANDMA.   Do we know these people on the floor?

LETTIE LU.   *(Annoyed to explain it again.)* We met 'em in town, Momma, Jake and Harry tied 'em up, and I read in the Bible that God wanted somebody to kill 'em.

GRANDMA.   *(Understanding.)* Oh.

LETTIE LU.   Well, I'm gonna sign off now. Read your Bible,

follow everything it says. And next week, we're gonna do the part from the Book of Leviticus about how to sacrifice turtle doves to please God.

GRANDMA.   Where we gonna get a turtle dove?

LETTIE LU.   You're really awake now, aren't you, Momma? I don't know. Maybe Woolworths'll have one of those 98 cents parakeets and then I'll kill that.

GRANDMA.   Kill the parakeet?

LETTIE LU.   That's what it says in the Bible. God, you can't follow anything, it's amazing I grew up to be as smart as I am. Good-bye, all! God bless you! Tune in next week for more readings from the Book of Leviticus Show! *(Lettie Lu waves at the camera. So does Grandma, though she looks back at the dead bodies a bit too. Music. Lights down.)*

PROPERTY LIST

Sign: BOOK OF LEVITICUS SHOW (LETTIE LU)
Bible (LETTIE LU)
Gun (LETTIE LU)

AUTHOR'S NOTE

Afterword

When did Anita Bryant have her anti-gay campaign in Florida? Late 70s? It's around then that I wrote the first version of this playlet.

As a Catholic growing up in the 50s, I was not that much encouraged to read the Bible by my church. You knew the gospels and the epistles because they were read on Sundays at Mass. And you knew selected passages that the church thought were important. But the Catholic Church, in the past at least, liked to "interpret" the Bible for you. So there was lots of the Bible I was extremely ignorant of.

For instance, the Book of Leviticus. Starting with Anita Bryant, the Christian right-wing often liked to quote the Book of Leviticus, from the Old Testament, to prove that "God" had said that homosexuality was wrong and a sin. And then to use that "fact" to try to keep homosexuals from teaching school, and to block the creation of any laws to protect homosexuals from being evicted or fired on the basis of prejudice against them. Basically, the Christian right says: prejudice against the homosexual is right!

So I thought I should read the Book of Leviticus. And I was appalled. There is a lot that is debatable in the Bible, and hard to understand ... but this particular book is preposterously out of date, and everyone, including the Christian right, ignores most of what's in it.

The Book of Leviticus is from the 7th century B.C., and it contains many lists of rules that I assume made sense to the people back then. It told you how to sacrifice turtle doves and bullocks in order to please God, or atone for a sin. You've sinned? Kill an animal! That'll fix it.

The Book is the basis for the Jewish dietary laws. Here's an example of its dietary rules: "These are the beasts ye shall eat ... whatsoever parteth the hoof, and is cloven-footed, and cheweth the cud, among the beasts, that shall ye eat. Nevertheless these shall ye not eat of them that chew the cud, but divideth not the hoof: the hare, because he cheweth the cud, but divideth not the hoof; he is unclean to you." Etc. Does the Christian right follow *this* part of the Book?

And it has this useful advice for how to behave around a woman who is menstruating: "And if a woman have an issue, and her issue in her flesh be blood, she shall be put apart seven days ... and whatsoever she sitteth upon shall be unclean ... and whosoever touches those things shall be unclean, and shall wash his clothes, and bathe himself in water, and be unclean until the even."

Now, that means if a woman has her period and she sits in a chair and then a man should happen to touch the chair, he must go wash his clothes and bathe and decide he (and she) are unclean. Right?

And *this* is the book from the Bible that people want to base public policy and public morality on?

These laws are from an ancient book in the Old Testament. Christ is quoted in the New Testament as saying He came to *complete* the law of Abraham ... that the Old Testament says "an eye for an eye," but that Christ says not to resist the evil doer, but to turn the other cheek.

Oh, no, let's not remember that passage. Let's look at this loony book about killing animals to please God, and who chews the cud and who doesn't, and let's base our morality on that!

The next time somebody quotes the Book of Leviticus to "prove" anything, don't let them get away with it. Demand consistency — demand they follow everything in the ludicrous book, not just the one sentence about condemning homosexuals (and adulterers; both are crimes worthy of death, according to Leviticus).

If there is a God, I believe He-She created evolution, and we're meant to move forward, evolving morally and emotionally (and we're clearly evolving in terms of technology); and I think Christ, God or just a teacher, was a being much evolved beyond the rest of his contemporaries. If we're to follow Christ, I think we're meant to follow his moral evolution, his completing and going beyond the law of Abraham. I find the idea of evolution to be greatly comforting, suggesting that there is forward motion, progress, hope.

To make use of a 7th century B.C. document, part of the Bible or not, in order to keep hardened prejudices and illogical fears in place is very un-Christ-like, in my opinion; not to mention dispiriting.

About the play — I created a character named Lettie Lu, who finds comfort in the Bible. I've had two actresses play her — my classmate friend from Yale, Kate McGregor-Stewart, who did it years ago on film for a prospective TV project; and Becky Ann Baker, who performed it in 1994 on video to be used as part of DURANG/DURANG. Both Kate and Becky were brilliant in their acting of Lettie Lu.

I wrote it originally for camera, and meant for it to be filmed in that home-made public access kind of way, with weird zooms and no cuts, and so on. For DURANG/DURANG I re-wrote it so it could be done onstage, though the director decided to shoot it for camera anyway, feeling it would be an interesting addition to a theatre evening. Either way is fine with me.

ENTERTAINING MR. HELMS

ENTERTAINING MR. HELMS was originally written in 1990 for a "one minute play" benefit for the American Repertory Theatre in Cambridge, Massachusetts (though it's more like six minutes).

Then it was performed again at a benefit for People for the American Way, in support of Harvey Gantt, who was running for the Senate against Mr. Helms. (Gantt lost, unfortunately, though he made a good showing.) At that benefit the rather star-studded cast for this sketch was:

FATHER ....Stephen Collins
MOTHER ....Sigourney Weaver
SON ....Jace Alexander
DAUGHTER ....Danitra Vance

The sketch had the following introduction:

PERSON.   In 1989 Senator Jesse Helms of North Carolina pushed through legislation by which anyone who won a grant that year from the National Endowment for the Arts would have to sign a statement promising that they would produce no work that was obscene, including promises to refrain from (quote) "depictions of sado-masochism, homoeroticism, the sexual exploitation of children, or individuals engaged in sex acts" (unquote).

Although only a maniac would be in favor of sexual exploitation of children, following the other requirements would preclude works like Jean Genet's THE BALCONY, Michelangelo's statue of David, and the final chapter, at least, of James Joyce's ULYSSES.

However, Mr. Helms undoubtedly knows best, and so this following piece was written at the time to try to please him. It is our hope to neither upset nor to offend anyone. Not any any any any any any one.

The scene is the kitchen of an American home at breakfast time. Mother, father, two children of either sex. Sorry — scratch "either sex." Mother, father, daughter, son.

(If you wish to use the introduction, it can be done live by an actor, or done over the speaker system. Or if you wish to dispense with the introduction, perhaps you could explain the "Helms connection" in a program note. Or you can just do the sketch as it is, and let the title be slightly mysterious.)

ENTERTAINING MR. HELMS

Scene: A sunny, happy kitchen in a sunny, happy American home. Father, Mother, Son, Daughter.

MOTHER. Good morning, John. Good morning, Jane.
SON. Good morning, Mother.
DAUGHTER. Good morning, Mother.
SON and DAUGHTER. Good morning, Father.
FATHER. Good morning. Hands on heart. *(Everyone places their hands on their hearts.)*
ALL OF THEM. I pledge allegiance to the flag
  Of the United States of America
  And to the republic for which it stands
  One nation, under God,
  Indivisible, with liberty and justice for all.
FATHER. Amen. Note if you will, it says "one nation, under God." It doesn't say under Satan, it doesn't say under agnostic. It says under *God.*
SON. Yes, Father.
DAUGHTER. Yes, Father.
MOTHER. Now here's your delicious breakfast — breakfast is the most important meal of the day.
DAUGHTER. Why doesn't Daddy ever make breakfast?
MOTHER. Daddy makes the money to pay for the breakfast, and mommy cooks it. That's how every single family in the United States is, and that's how the men and the women were in the Bible also. And please don't ask that question again.
DAUGHTER. All right, Mommy.
FATHER. What are you learning in your public schools that my tax money pays for, I'd like to know. John?
SON. Well in science class we're learning that it took God six days to make the world, and on the seventh day He rested. And we're learning that disease came about because Adam and Eve disobeyed God.

FATHER. I'm happy to hear this. This science teacher sounds much better than your previous one, who I got fired.

MOTHER. "Whom" I got fired, dear.

FATHER. Oh, you're right. Thank you, darling. Children, listen to your mother when she speaks about grammar or cooking.

MOTHER. The trick to making a three-minute egg is to cook it for 2 minutes and 45 seconds.

FATHER. Ask me about arithmetic, however. And about morals. And about sports. John, how is gym class going?

SON. Great, Dad. We played basketball yesterday, and one team was shirts, and the other team was skins, and I was on the skins team, and we ...

MOTHER. John, dear, don't talk about young men with their shirts off please, dear. We don't want to give the audience homoerotic ideas. Just say team A and team B.

SON. Oh. Okay. Team A and team B; and then team B won.

FATHER. Well, that's splendid.

SON. Then we took our clothes off in the locker room, and we took showers.

MOTHER. John!

SON. Well, we were sweaty.

MOTHER. John, go to your room.

SON. What did I say?

FATHER. John, you heard your mother.

SON. All right. *(Exits.)*

MOTHER. I hope there's nothing wrong with him. You know, Freud said there was a latency period.

FATHER. Elizabeth, my God, don't talk about Freud. I'm sure John is fine. If he's not fine, we'll put him through aversion therapy. And if that doesn't work, we'll disown him.

DAUGHTER. What are you two talking about? All he said was his team won at basketball.

MOTHER. It was how he said it, darling. And don't call your parents "you two." Say mother and father. Or mater and pater.

DAUGHTER. Yes, Mater and Pater.

FATHER.   Well, Jane, how is home economics going?

DAUGHTER. Fine, except that Amy was hemorraghing the

other day.

MOTHER. Really? Was it part of a class project?

DAUGHTER. No, Mom, she had a homemade abortion because she was afraid to talk to her parents to get their permission for a regular one.

FATHER. What's being said? I don't like this.

DAUGHTER. Don't worry, Daddy, it'll never happen to me. Amy's a regular slut because she's such an emotional mess she keeps looking for love from boys and she doesn't know about contraception because you got our health teacher fired.

FATHER. That woman was giving students a blueprint for prostitution.

DAUGHTER. But that's just Amy, it won't happen to me. And you know why?

MOTHER. Why, dear?

DAUGHTER. Because I love you and Daddy, and I will always obey you, and I will never give the preciousness of my body to any boy until we're married and ready and capable of having a baby. I am a good girl, and I am pure. And I'm against abortion, and if only it was against the law, I would gladly turn my friend Amy into the authorities, so she'd be put in jail if she wasn't already dead.

MOTHER. Oh, we have raised a wonderful daughter.

FATHER. We certainly have. I thank God for her. Thank you, Jesus.

MOTHER. Jesus? Darling, I thought we were Jewish.

FATHER. We were. But I've been thinking about Jesus a lot lately, and so many people I admire believe in him — Oliver North, John Poindexter, John Cardinal O'Connor. And I think it's time we converted. Enough of this chosen people business. The true chosen people are the Christians! Tomorrow morning after we say the Pledge of Allegiance, I want you all to have memorized the "Our Father."

MOTHER. Oh. Well, this is a bit of a shift for me. And I think it will upset my parents. But you're my husband, and I love to obey you, and you know best in everything. *(Mother and Father kiss.)*

FATHER. I certainly do. I don't understand why everyone

doesn't agree with me all the time. I think all this disparity of opinion in our country is confusing to our children, and a great big waste of time. America works for me perfectly — I believe in God, I believe in prayer, I believe in military preparedness, I believe in heterosexuality, I believe in the authority of parents over their children, I believe in putting your toys away when you're done with them, I believe in knowing what's right, and doing what's right, and making sure everyone else knows and does what's right. To me, there is no room for difference of opinion when you're *right*. Am I right?

MOTHER.   You're right, darling. When you're right, you're right.

DAUGHTER.   You're right, Dad. You're far right! And I'm proud of you for it. Oh how I love my parents and my country. *(Enter son.)*

SON.   Dad, I'm sorry for what I said before. And I'm joining the Army. I want to be just like Oliver North.

MOTHER.   Oh, this is a happy day! We've become Christians, our daughter has told us she'll save her body until marriage, and now our son wants to join the military. To live in America is perfection! Who could ask for anything more? *(Mother and Father kiss. Son and Daughter smile and look on.)*

AFTERWORD

Mother's line "We don't want to give the audience homoerotic ideas" can be changed to "We don't want to give anyone homoerotic ideas" if you would prefer not to refer to the audience during the sketch (since the characters mostly don't). I personally don't mind referring to the audience, and then not returning to it; but change the line if you wish.

THE DOCTOR WILL
SEE YOU NOW

THE DOCTOR WILL SEE YOU NOW was done onstage in New York City as part of a political revue produced by the Acting Company called ISSUE? I DON'T EVEN KNOW YOU. The cast was as follows:

WOMAN SINGER ....Mary Lou Rosato
MR. NELSON ....Casey Biggs
NURSE CALLIOPE ....Kristine Nielson
DR. MURGATROYD ....Wayne Knight

CHARACTERS

WOMAN SINGER, happy and loud
MR. NELSON, the patient
NURSE CALLIOPE, the nurse
DR. MURGATROYD, the doctor

THE DOCTOR WILL
SEE YOU NOW

Scene: A Woman Singer appears in a spotlight. She is dressed in a garish sequined dress with a flashy show biz boa, as if she were a guest on some awful TV variety show. She sings a strident, up-beat song about the glories of love. She sings to the audience loudly, selling the song too hard, and energetically.

After she sings a bit she says to audience:

WOMAN SINGER.
It's not just love that's sweeping the country.
Love isn't just from the neck up,
So best be safe, and get a check-up!
(She sings the end tag line of the song. She smiles delightedly.)
MAN'S VOICE.   The preceding has been a public service announcement. *(Lights out on her.)*
Scene: A doctor's waiting room, R.; and a doctor's office, L. The waiting room setting takes up less space; the doctor's office is bigger. At present only the waiting room part of the set is lit. In the waiting room is Mr. Wilson, a mild looking man. And there is a Nurse, who is quite pretty and personable. Also sitting in the waiting room is the Woman Singer from a moment ago. She is still in her cabaret show glittering gown and boa, and so looks very odd in this setting. Mr. Wilson is reading a magazine. The Woman Singer is sitting, but staring ahead, attentive. The Nurse is on the phone.)
NURSE.   *(Into phone.)* I'll bring him in, doctor. *(Gets up, crosses to Mr. Wilson.)* The doctor will see you now, Mr. Wilson. *(The Woman Singer bounds out of her seat and starts singing the same song she sang at the top of the piece. It is loud and sold very hard again.)* Please, Mrs. Malloway, stop doing that. It's nerve-racking.
WOMAN SINGER. *(Petulant, insistent.)* I want to see the doctor!
NURSE.   He's seen you already. There's nothing wrong with you. Physically. Besides, it's Mr. Wilson's appointment now.

WOMAN SINGER. I'm not leaving here until the doctor gives me ... medication! *(Stamps her foot, and smiles madly at the audience.)*

NURSE. I'll see what I can do. *(Woman Singer sits back down. Nurse leads Mr. Wilson toward L., speaks to him. To Wilson, friendly.)* She's really a nut case, I'm afraid. The doctor has seen her twice already today, but she just won't go away.

MR. WILSON. It must be difficult for you.

NURSE. Yes. I never wanted to be a nurse. I wanted to be an encyclopedia salesman, but I couldn't carry the books. So I had to settle for this. Here's the doctor now. *(Nurse brings Mr. Wilson into the office of Doctor Murgatroyd; L. R. should fade into darkness, with the Woman Singer seated back in her chair.)* I'll just leave you two here. *(Exits.)*

DOCTOR. Fine woman. Reminds me of my mother. Hello, how are you feeling?

MR. WILSON. Well, all right. It's just the pollen count is very heavy right now, and as I said last week, my allergies have been bothering me.

DOCTOR. I see. Let me just look at your chart. *(Looks at it.)* Uh huh. Uh huh. Hmmmm. *(Looks up at him.)* I think I know what's bothering you.

MR. WILSON. It isn't allergies?

DOCTOR. No. It's VD. *(Woman Singer bursts into the room, run after by the Nurse. Woman Singer sings her "Love" song at the top of her lungs, aiming it at the Doctor and Mr. Wilson and the audience.)*

NURSE. I'm sorry, doctor. She got away from me. Come along, Mrs. Malloway. *(Nurse drags out Woman Singer.)*

DOCTOR. That woman has strong lungs. No smoking there.

MR. WILSON. I don't understand. I couldn't have VD. There's just me and my wife, and I haven't, and she hasn't ...

DOCTOR. Please give me a list of all recent contacts you've had. By state law we have to inform them that they may be infected. *(Hands him a form.)* There's room for 80 names and phone numbers. If you need more space, I'll give you another form.

MR. WILSON. There haven't been any contacts. Do you have the right chart in front of you? I came to you last week for my allergies. I've been sneezing.

DOCTOR. *(To intercom.)* Nurse Calliope, would you come in here please? *(To Mr. Wilson.)* Now, do you have a pen?

MR. WILSON. I think there's been a mistake.

DOCTOR. If you're unwilling to name names, by state law we are allowed to confiscate your address book, and call everyone in it. *(The Nurse enters during the above and goes behind Mr. Wilson's chair.)*

NURSE. Is he ticklish? *(She tickles him, and at the same time removes his address book from his jacket pocket. Mr. Wilson squirms with the tickling.)*

MR. WILSON. Stop that!

NURSE. Here it is! *(Takes his address book away.)*

DOCTOR. Now we'll start you on penicillin ...

MR. WILSON. But I'm allergic to penicillin.

DOCTOR. Mr. Wilson, venereal disease is a national concern and a public disgrace. Please do not fight me on this.

NURSE. How do you think he got it? *(Doctor whispers to her.)* Oh, bad Mr. Wilson. Shall I call his wife? *(Looks at his chart, dials the phone.)*

MR. WILSON. I think you have my chart confused.

NURSE. Well, let's see who answers the phone. I got the number from your chart. *(To phone.)* Hello, Mrs. Wilson? *(To Mr. Wilson.)* She said yes. *(To phone.)* Mrs. Wilson, this is Nurse Calliope from Doctor Murgatroyd's office. By state law we have to inform you that you have been named as a possible contact by someone who has venereal disease. What? No, that's not the name. *(Laughs; to Mr. Wilson.)* She thought it was someone else. Who's Gregory? *(To phone.)* No, Mrs. Wilson, it's your husband. Please make an appointment to see your physician as soon as possible. VD is a national problem. Did you know that there are 200 teenage pregnancies every five minutes? *(During the above the Doctor has been taking Mr. Wilson's blood pressure, taking his temperature, otherwise keeping him involved. Mr. Wilson finally pulls away and goes to the Nurse.)*

MR. WILSON. Give me the phone please. *(He reaches for the phone; Nurse slaps his hand.)*

NURSE. Grabby. That's the kind of behavior that got you in

this mess. *(To phone.)* That's right. Every five minutes. *(Hangs up.)*

DOCTOR.   Are your parents still living?

MR. WILSON.   Yes, they are.

DOCTOR.   We have to call them. Nurse, find the number. *(Nurse looks through book.)*

MR. WILSON.   This has gone for enough.

DOCTOR.   No, Mr. Wilson, it is you who have gone far enough. You went too far, and you must pay the consequences. Now, according to the government, I must by law inform the parents of anyone who wishes to purchase birth control or who has a venereal disease. *(To Nurse.)* Have you found their number yet?

NURSE.   *(Looking through book.)* I'm still looking. Oooh, he knows Barry Manilow, I love him.

MR. WILSON.   It's a different Barry Manilow. Doctor, I know the President *supported* a law about telling parents of teenagers about if they ever wanted to get birth control, you know, a parental consent kind of law, I think, but it was never made into law, the congress didn't pass it ...

NURSE.   *(Looking at watch.)* Ooops. There goes another teenage pregnancy.

MR. WILSON.   But even if they did pass it, I think you have the law confused. Surely the President doesn't mean for you to call up the parents of *adults*.

DOCTOR.   That is my understanding of the matter.

NURSE.   Oh, I found them. They're in a retirement village. *(Starts to dial.)*

MR. WILSON.   But you'll just upset them. And besides, I have an allergy, I don't have venereal disease.

DOCTOR.   Mr. Wilson, if you have lived a degraded life and have disgraced yourself by Lord knows what disgusting activities, at least be man enough not to deny it. Moral laxity is a national disgrace in our country, and the President and I, not to mention the House and Senate, *refuse* to put up with it. Isn't that so, Nurse Calliope?

NURSE.   Right. *(Into phone.)* Hello, is this Mrs. Wilson, the mother of Arthur Wilson?

MR. WILSON.   Give me that phone. *(Doctor holds up a hypodermic.)*

DOCTOR.   You interfere with procedure, and by law I will be forced to inject you.

MR. WILSON.   What?

DOCTOR.   You heard me.

NURSE.   *(Into phone.)* Mrs. Wilson, I'm afraid I'm calling you about a family disgrace. Your son Arthur has that bad disease that begins with the letter "v."

MR. WILSON.   This is insane.

NURSE.   No, Mrs. Wilson, not venous thrombosis. *(Laughs; to the room.)* What a nut. *(To phone.)* The first word rhymes with cereal.

MR. WILSON.   Mother, hang up. This is the beginning of fascism.

DOCTOR.   That's a rude and inflammatory remark. Now I'm going to *have* to inject you. *(Doctor jabs him with needle; Mr. Wilson falls over.)*

MR. WILSON.   *(Fading, falling.)* I … just …wanted … a simple anti-histamine.

NURSE.   No, Mrs. Wilson, I don't mean Wheaties. It rhymes with the word "cereal," not with the brand name of a cereal. *(To Doctor.)* I think she must be quite elderly. This may take a long time. *(To phone.)* Starts with a "v." Uh huh. *(Nurse makes a face at the Doctor as if to say "Isn't this fun?" The Doctor smiles back, and listens into the phone too, sharing the earpiece with the nurse.)* Yes, the second letter is a vowel…. Uh huh. Uh huh. *(The lights fade on the Nurse and the Doctor on the phone, but not to black. The Woman Singer enters and stands in front of the scene in a bright spot. She sings some more of her "Love" song again, then addresses the audience.)*

WOMAN SINGER.   La da da da, la da da da da … *(Spoken.)* It's sweeping the country. But don't sweep it under the carpet. We care about you. And so does your government. But remember, freedom has its limits. No one has the right to yell "fire" in a crowded theatre, and no one has the right to play "Bolero" in the privacy of his or her own bedroom either. We can't let you make your own decision. You're not smart enough. But don't worry. We're smart, and we'll do it for you! *(She smiles delightedly, and sings the final line of the "Love" song she had been singing.)*

MAN'S VOICE.   The preceding has been a public service announcement. *(End play.)*

PROPERTY LIST

Medical form (DOCTOR)
Address book (NURSE)
Hypodermic needle (DOCTOR)

AUTHOR'S NOTE

Afterword

I wrote this sketch sometime during the Reagan years, first for a TV sketch show, where it wasn't produced, and then for a political cabaret with the Acting Company, where it was produced.

Sex education and access to birth control information was and is a hot potato with the religious right. During the Reagan and Bush years, the Republicans were always trying to push through bills and laws limiting freedom in those areas.

During the Bush years we had the "gag" rule, whereby any public health worker or doctor working in a tax-supported clinic could not even mention the word "abortion" to a woman, even though it is still a legal right. This is because the right wing doesn't want a penny of its money to go to something it disagrees with, legal or not, private decision or not.

During the Reagan years, there was a lot of talk about "parental notification" — that if a woman under 18 wanted an abortion she would have to get her parents' signed permission; or if a woman under 18 wanted birth control, she would have to get her parents' signed permission.

One's attitude to these sorts of things so much depends not only on one's morality, but on one's imagination, on what kind of family scenario one conjures up.

For the religious right, it seems, they think of some strong-willed teenage girl disobeying her strong, good, moral parents. She tries to get birth control, and by law her parents are notified. Then the parents sit her down and say: "Stephanie, we are shocked and mortified! What are you thinking of? You must be abstinent and save yourself until marriage as your mother did in 1941." At which point Stephanie says, "Thank you, mother and father. How I love you. I can't imagine what I was thinking of trying to be sexual. I am a nut. But no more. I bask in your parental wisdom and love, and from now on, I will save myself until marriage." And, thus, in that scenario, the parental consent laws are a good idea.

In my scenario, having grown up around lots of alcoholism, I envision a girl whose alcoholic father flies into rages and beats her. She's desperate for attention, and so she hooks up with a boyfriend who wants to have sex. She wants birth control in order to keep from having a baby. When she tries to get the birth control, the parental notification law kicks in, they call up her father, he flies into a rage, he beats her; she runs to the arms of her boyfriend for comfort, and she gets pregnant, and some poor child is dragged into this world to be brought up by this too young, unstable woman. And that's my scenario.

Anyway, this sketch was an absurdist one triggered by attempts in the Reagan years to write "parental notification" laws into any tax-funded family clinic that offered birth control devices to people under age 18.

UNDER DURESS:
Words on Fire

UNDER DURESS was part of WORDS ON FIRE, a program of pieces on fire or heat. It aired on PBS on ALIVE FROM OFF-CENTER in late 1990. It was produced by Wendall Harrington, and directed by John Sanborn. The cast was as follows:

CHRIS ....Christopher Durang
STEPHANIE..Kristine Nielson
PHOTOGRAPHER..Peter Cunningham
BOY SCOUT ....Charles Steinmann

AUTHOR'S NOTE

This piece was written for camera. I have done a quick rewrite to make it playable on stage (though you need to use slides).

CHARACTERS

CHRIS
STEPHANIE, his trendy friend
BOY SCOUT (in slide)

UNDER DURESS:
Words on Fire

Scene: A comfortable living room, morning. Chris, a 30-ish author, addresses the audience.

Sitting on a couch behind him, waiting for the scene to begin, is Stephanie, an intense woman. She is dressed somewhat trendily.

CHRIS.   Hello. How are you. I was remembering those four years we had with President George Bush, and a conversation I had with my friend Stephanie. So let's go back to that time. *(Chris crosses to his couch, and sits down to speak with Stephanie.)* Hello, Stephanie.

STEPHANIE.   Hello, Chris. How's your writing going?

CHRIS.   Oh you know.

STEPHANIE.   Yes. An artist's life.

CHRIS.   *(Uncomfortable with talk of art.)* Yes. Um … *(Changes topic.)* You know, I was reading this editorial in the paper about global warming, and how President Bush isn't doing anything about it even though all of his advisors, except one, have said he should do something right away, you know, about the emissions that cause global warming. But he's not doing anything. And then I had this dream about being really, really hot on the earth, and not being able to breathe. And things kept catching on fire. Do you think I should write him a letter? Or is it all pointless?

STEPHANIE.   I was reading *The Psychoanalysis of Fire* by Gaston Bachelard the other day.

CHRIS.   Oh yes?

STEPHANIE.   And I wrote down this quote to tell you, I thought it was so true. If I can just find it in my purse. *(Goes through purse.)*

CHRIS.   I've never heard of this book. Is it famous?

STEPHANIE.   Well, it's not on the best seller list. Ah, here it is. Listen to this. "It is impossible to escape this dialectic: to be aware that one is burning is to grow cold; to feel an intensity is to diminish it; it is necessary to be an intensity without realizing it. Such is the bitter law of man's activity." *(Looks at him significantly.)*

CHRIS.   I'm sorry, I just got up a little while ago. Can you say it again?

STEPHANIE.   Maybe I didn't read it right. Let me do it again, emphasizing different words. *(Stressing words oddly.)* "It is *impossible* to escape this *dialectic:* to be aware that one is *burning* is to grow *cold;* to *feel* an *intensity* is to *diminish* it; it is necessary to *be an intensity* without realizing it. *Without realizing it.* Such is the bitter law of man's activity. Such is the *bitter* law ... *(Makes "bitter taste" faces.)* ... of man's activity."

CHRIS.   I don't know if I really followed it.

STEPHANIE.   Maybe I should do it again.

CHRIS.   No, please, don't. Let me look at it, I can't hear it aloud, I don't think. *(Looks at it.)* What is "dialectic" again? Two opposing thoughts or something?

STEPHANIE.   Didn't you read Marx? He used the word "dialectic" constantly.

CHRIS.   I didn't read Marx. I went to Catholic school.

STEPHANIE.   Oh. Well, "dialectic" means ... "ideas, thoughts ..." "coming to ideas by logic." I think. Let's move past that word.

CHRIS.   Uh huh. "To be aware one is burning is to grow cold." All right, he's not talking about actually being burned, like with boiling water, right? I've been burned, it isn't to grow cold.

STEPHANIE.   No, I don't think Gaston means actually being burned. I think he means to be burning in an intellectual sense — like having a "fever of ideas."

CHRIS.   *(Trying to make sense.)* All right, a fever of ideas. When you are in a fever of ideas and you are aware of it, you grow cold — and the fever of ideas dwindles down to a ... trickle of cool, non-feverish ideas.

STEPHANIE.   Well, less elegantly, but yes.

CHRIS.   *(Reads again.)* "To feel an intensity is to diminish it; it is necessary to be an intensity without realizing it." So when you're fired up with an idea, or feeling, and you start to be conscious about it, the passion you feel diminishes because of this consciousness, and so ... *(Cranky, frustrated.)* And so *what?* This thought is so abstract it makes me want to scream.

STEPHANIE. Well, you're reading it out of context.

CHRIS. Is the whole book this way?

STEPHANIE. If I had known you were an anti-intellectual, I wouldn't have taken the quote out of my purse. *(They sit in silence for a moment.)*

CHRIS. So, do you think I should write George Bush?

STEPHANIE. What about?

CHRIS. This global warming thing.

STEPHANIE. I really couldn't say.

CHRIS. Well, don't be mad about the quote, Stephanie.

STEPHANIE. I will be mad about it. I make perfectly good conversation, then *you* do an endless dialectic, and you make me feel ... stupid.

CHRIS. You're not stupid. I just couldn't follow the quote.

STEPHANIE. Yes, you made that evident.

CHRIS. Let's talk about something else.

STEPHANIE. What, global warming? Your topic?

CHRIS. It's not my topic. But it's really serious. I mean, if the scientists are right and temperatures go up and stay up, then the polar caps will melt and the sea levels will rise, and there'll be famine and disease and death for our children.

STEPHANIE. We don't have children.

CHRIS. Well, for other people's children.

STEPHANIE. Well, I have to go now.

CHRIS. Oh, all right. Thanks for coming by.

STEPHANIE. You're welcome. Will I see you at Pamela's opening?

CHRIS. Who's Pamela?

STEPHANIE. I guess I won't. Good-bye.

CHRIS. I'll see you to the door. *(Chris walks her to the door of his apartment, opens the door.)* Good-bye.

STEPHANIE. Good-bye. *(She exits. Chris looks back to the audience.)*

CHRIS. *(To audience.)* I guess I upset Stephanie. I didn't mean to. Maybe if I read the quote in another mood, I would've liked it. I found it hard to understand. Excuse me, I'm going to try to write this letter to the President. *(Lights dim. The sound of typing. On a screen we see projected a few slides of Chris typing a letter at his computer. He looks intense, focused. The sound of typing stops. Lights back up on Chris, holding his finished letter, sealed in an envelope. He waves the letter in his hand.)*

(To audience.) Well, I finished it. *(Looks at it, thoughtfully.)*

Now the problem with the letter is that it's in sentences. And judging from the presidential campaign, maybe George Bush only understands sound bytes. *(Thinks.)*

I don't know that he'll follow it. Maybe I better redo this letter in sound-bytes, and with photo opportunities. I better find a photographer. *(Lights change. On the screen we see a slide of Chris shaking hands with a photographer, then of posing in front of a photographer's white backdrop. Then we see a series of slides of Chris in poses, while the real Chris stands nearby reciting his sound bytes. First pose in slide: Chris dressed in suit, looking respectable. But holding his collar out, as if it's hot.)*

(Live.) Hey, George! Earth hot! *(Moves his collar back and forth, fans his face, makes uncomfortable faces. Second pose in slide: Chris stands by nine-year-old Boy Scout. Chris has hand on Boy Scout's head, paternal.)*

(Live.) George: strong leader needed! *(Third pose in slide: Chris dressed as fireman, with heavy fireman coat and helmet.)*

(Live.) Don't risk future inferno! *(Fourth pose in slide: Chris, back in suit, in front of many, many candles, either on a table or on a birthday cake.)*

(Live. With urgency.) Thousand points of light, heating up! Fire fire fire! *(Fifth pose in slide: Chris, still in suit, but wearing a Carmen Miranda fruit hat and earrings for some reason.)*

(Live.) Don't wait, act now. *(Sixth pose in slide: Chris, just in suit again, holding Monopoly play money in one hand, and a plastic balloon globe of the world in another.)*

(Live.) Which more important — money or continuation of planet? *(Seventh pose in slide: Chris seated on ground next to a sweet looking dalmation dog. The dalmation looks placid and has a letter in his mouth.)*

(Live.) Dear George. Letter to follow. *(The slide show is finished. Lights off screen. Lights focus back more clearly on Chris in living room.)*

(To audience.) Wow. That was exhausting. And I think the photographer's bill will be large. And who knows if Bush will understand what I've said; you can't really make an argument in sound bytes. I should really just send the original letter I wrote, and forget about the sound bytes. *(Looks down at the envelope.)*

Oh. But I need to buy a stamp. Ohhhhhh. *(Spirals down into depression.)*

Uhhhhhhh, and the lines in the post office are so long. It'll take hours. And sometimes the postal employees go crazy and shoot people, and he probably will never read the letter anyway, and what can just one person do, it all seems so hopeless. Maybe I should just forget the letter. Maybe I'll be *dead* before the global warming thing gets bad enough. *(Deflates to nothing almost; then looks out at audience.)*

But that's no way to behave, is it? The individual does count, doesn't he? And even if he doesn't entirely, we have to act as if we do, don't we? I think so. Right. Right. *(Recaptures his energy and intention.)*

Okay, okay! I'm ready. I will go to the post office. I will buy the stamp. I will send the letter. Here I go. Good-bye! *(Chris waves good-bye to audience and leaves through his apartment door. The door shuts with purpose behind him. End play.)*

PROPERTY LIST

Purse with quotes paper (STEPHANIE)
Envelope with letter (CHRIS)

AUTHOR'S NOTE

Afterword

I was asked by producer Wendell Harrington to write a 10 minute piece for camera for a program on PBS called ALIVE FROM OFF-CENTER. This particular program was to be called WORDS ON FIRE, and each piece was meant somehow to be about "fire" or "heat." Or something like that.

I was told I could be in my piece if I wanted, and it seemed that it was actually going to get filmed. So I was intrigued. (And it did get filmed and aired. And it was fun to shoot.)

The piece I wrote featured myself and my fabulously talented actress friend Kristine Nielson, whom I had met several times over the years but whom I bonded with in 1989 when she and I were trapped together in an unfortunate production of Alfred Jarry's UBU at Lincoln Center. (She played the Queen, and I played UBU's Conscience, barefoot in a nightshirt.)

The concept of "heat" made me think of global warming; and at the time I wrote this piece (March, 1990), the United States had recently, under the presidency of George Bush, been the only major country to oppose proposals to cut emissions from gases that cause global warming at something called the Hague conference. And then in March this was followed by Bush, at the urging of John Sununu (and against the advice of many other of his advisers), making a speech belittling the need to make any changes to guard against global warming.

I know there doesn't seem to be consensus on global warming, but I find myself very frightened of the people, usually Republicans, who seem never to believe in global warming at all. On environmental issues they seem to make decisions related to what's best for business to make maximum money, and seemingly have no interest in whether the businesses are indeed polluting the air we breathe … and hope to keep breathing.

So anyway, that's the piece I've written. (Oh, and yes. I did write George Bush a letter at the time. Hmmmmmm.)

AN ALTAR BOY
TALKS TO GOD

(Adapted from a section of LAUGHING WILD)

AN ALTAR BOY TALKS TO GOD was first produced as part of A MESS OF PLAYS BY CHRIS DURANG at South Coast Repertory, in Costa Mesa, California. The evening was directed by David Chambers, and the cast for this piece was as follows:

ROBERT .... Robert Patrick Benedict
GOD .... Hal Landon, Jr.

CHARACTERS

ROBERT, a young man
GOD, God

AUTHOR'S NOTE

This piece is adapted from a section of the man's monologue in my full length play LAUGHING WILD, rewritten for two voices and with a new introductory section. In LAUGHING WILD, the Man plays both God and an angel, talking back and forth, about whether God really created AIDs as a "punishment" (a frequently said thing early in the AIDs epidemic).

For the purposes of the South Coast Repertory evening of plays, David Chambers and I decided that the God-angel dialogue could work out of context. And when I met the young actor Robert Patrick Benedict who was to play the angel debating God, I decided to rewrite it to suit him more and to ease the audience into the piece.

Happily, fewer people get away with saying that AIDs is a punishment from God these days. Oddly, though, the notion that God "punishes" us through misfortune and diseases is a hard one for people to get out of their psyches ... and so the piece still seems germane to me. Do you like the word "germane"?

Oh, a stray pronunciation note: The Mass in Latin is so far gone, and Robert has to make reference to it ... so to help you: the Latin phrase "Kyrie Eleison" is pronounced "Keer-ee-ā Ā-lay-ee-son." And "Et cum spiritu tuo" is pronounced: "ett cum speer-ee-too too-oh."

AN ALTAR BOY
TALKS TO GOD

Scene: Robert, a young man, comes out and stands in a spotlight. He talks directly to the audience. He is friendly and outgoing with them.

ROBERT. I used to be an altar boy; from about age 8 to age 14. I used to ring the little bell when the priest would hold up the Eucharist. And I used to swing the little iron pot thing that was filled with incense when it was Lent. And I used to hand the priest things ... like a holy napkin to wipe his mouth after he drank the wine that wasn't just wine, but was Christ's blood transubstantiated.

I'm sort of sorry I wasn't an altar boy back when it was all in Latin. I have an older brother who's like 20 years older than me ... 'cause I'm the youngest of 8 children, and so the age spread in our family is really big; I have a couple of nephews who are older than me ... do you follow that?

Anyway, this older brother of mine said it was a lot more exciting to be an altar boy back when it was in Latin. The priest would say "Kyrie Eleison," and then you'd say back, "Et cum spiritu tuo." And now instead the priest says, "The Lord be with you," and then the whole congregation, not just the altar boy, says "And also with you."

But, like, nobody in their right mind says, "And also with you." It sounds like you're talking from a foreign language dictionary. I mean, you might say, "And you too." Or "Thanks, buddy, same to you." But you don't say "And also with you."

So anyway, I missed the whole church in Latin thing, but it sounded interesting.

And then I stopped being an altar boy at about age 14 because I was on the swim team and I practiced so much I didn't want to have to get up for 8 A.M. mass on Sunday. So I went to twelve noon mass with my parents and with some of my nephews, who are older than me.

And then one of these nephews got AIDs. It was very hush hush. It was early in the epidemic, and people didn't know much about it except it was really awful and that if you got it through a blood transfusion or because you were a hemophiliac, well, then, that wasn't so bad, I mean, nothing to be ashamed of. But if you got it from using a hypodermic to shoot drugs or because of some sexual act you shouldn't be doing, well then, this was considered embarrassing, and you and your parents should only talk in a whisper.

And then some fundamentalist-type people started to say that God had sent AIDs as a punishment to gay people. And I thought to myself, wow ... this doesn't fit my idea of God. So I went to heaven, and I asked God what it all meant. *(The stage changes. A curtain opens, or lights shift, and we see GOD seated in a lounge chair, drinking an iced tea or something. GOD is an older man, a bit cranky, wearing a loose robe. Robert goes up to GOD.)*

Hello, God.

GOD.   Hello, who are you?

ROBERT.   I used to be an altar boy.

GOD.   Oh yes, hello.

ROBERT.   What can you tell me about AIDs and gay people?

GOD.   Boy oh boy, do I hate homosexuals. And so I've given them a really horrifying disease.

ROBERT.   *(Surprised.)* Really?

GOD.   Yes. And drug addicts ... and hemophiliacs.

ROBERT.   But why hemophiliacs?

GOD.   Oh, no reason. I want the disease to go through the bloodstream, and I can't figure out how to send the disease through the bloodstream and not affect hemophiliacs.

ROBERT.   Yes, but aren't you all powerful, can't you make the disease just hit the people you want it to hit?

GOD.   Well, you'd think I could, but I can't seem to. And so if hemophiliacs get it, well ... the suffering will be good for them.

ROBERT.   Really? In what way?

GOD.   Oh, I don't know. I'll explain it at the end of the world.

ROBERT.   I see. Tell me, what about the children of drug addicts? Will they get the disease through their mother's wombs?

GOD. *(Suddenly realizing this.)* Well — why not? Serve the hophead mothers right. Boy oh boy, do I hate women drug addicts!

ROBERT. Yes, but why punish their babies?

GOD. And I hate homosexuals!

ROBERT. Yes, yes, we got you hate homosexuals ...

GOD. Except for Noel Coward, he was droll ...

ROBERT. Yes, he was droll.

GOD. And I hate Haitians! Anything beginning with the letter "h."

ROBERT. Goodness. But isn't it unfair to infect innocent babies in the womb with this dreadful disease?

GOD. Look, homosexuals and drug addicts are very very bad people; and if babies get it, well, don't forget I'm God, so you better just presume I have some secret reason why it's good they get it too.

ROBERT. Yes, but what is this secret reason?

GOD. Stop asking so many questions ...

ROBERT. Yes, but ...

GOD. There you go again, trying to horn in on the Tree of Knowledge just like Adam and Eve did. Boy oh boy does that make me wrathful!

Okay you ask me questions and irritate me, I'm going to give AIDs to 3,000 more homosexuals. Pow! How do you like that?

And 7,000 more drug addicts. Pow! And to little Mary Johnson in Hoboken, New Jersey, she's a hemophiliac, pow! And to a whole bunch of Haitians ... pow! pow!

Oh ... and I hereby revoke penicillin. Anyone out there who has ever been exposed to syphilis will suffer and die just like they used to — as a side issue, I love to connect sex and death, I don't know why I invented sex to begin with, it's a revolting idea, but as long as I have, I want it done *properly* in the *missionary* position with *one* person for life, or I want those who disobey me to die a horrible death from AIDs and syphilis and God knows what else. Is that clear?

ROBERT. Very clear. Well, good-bye. *(Robert walks to another area of light; lights dim on the area God is in.)* Well, I don't think that was really God, do you? I think that was a rageaholic somewhere. Or a projected image of some really angry people. But it wasn't God, and it wasn't heaven. I think it's harder to get to heaven and talk to God than I thought.

PROPERTY LIST

Iced tea or other drink (GOD)

NEW PLAYS

★ **YELLOW FACE by David Henry Hwang.** Asian-American playwright DHH leads a protest against the casting of Jonathan Pryce as the Eurasian pimp in the original Broadway production of *Miss Saigon*, condemning the practice as "yellowface." The lines between truth and fiction blur with hilarious and moving results in this unreliable memoir. "A pungent play of ideas with a big heart." *–Variety.* "Fabulously inventive." *–The New Yorker.* [5M, 2W] ISBN: 978-0-8222-2301-6

★ **33 VARIATIONS by Moisés Kaufmann.** A mother coming to terms with her daughter. A composer coming to terms with his genius. And, even though they're separated by 200 years, these two people share an obsession that might, even just for a moment, make time stand still. "A compellingly original and thoroughly watchable play for today." *–Talkin' Broadway.* [4M, 4W] ISBN: 978-0-8222-2392-4

★ **BOOM by Peter Sinn Nachtrieb.** A grad student's online personal ad lures a mysterious journalism student to his subterranean research lab. But when a major catastrophic event strikes the planet, their date takes on evolutionary significance and the fate of humanity hangs in the balance. "Darkly funny dialogue." *–NY Times.* "Literate, coarse, thoughtful, sweet, scabrously inappropriate." *–Washington City Paper.* [1M, 2W] ISBN: 978-0-8222-2370-2

★ **LOVE, LOSS AND WHAT I WORE by Nora Ephron and Delia Ephron, based on the book by Ilene Beckerman.** A play of monologues and ensemble pieces about women, clothes and memory covering all the important subjects—mothers, prom dresses, mothers, buying bras, mothers, hating purses and why we only wear black. "Funny, compelling." *–NY Times.* "So funny and so powerful." *–WowOwow.com.* [5W] ISBN: 978-0-8222-2355-9

★ **CIRCLE MIRROR TRANSFORMATION by Annie Baker.** When four lost New Englanders enrolled in Marty's community center drama class experiment with harmless games, hearts are quietly torn apart, and tiny wars of epic proportions are waged and won. "Absorbing, unblinking and sharply funny." *–NY Times.* [2M, 3W] ISBN: 978-0-8222-2445-7

★ **BROKE-OLOGY by Nathan Louis Jackson.** The King family has weathered the hardships of life and survived with their love for each other intact. But when two brothers are called home to take care of their father, they find themselves strangely at odds. "Engaging dialogue." *–TheaterMania.com.* "Assured, bighearted." *–Time Out.* [3M, 1W] ISBN: 978-0-8222-2428-0

DRAMATISTS PLAY SERVICE, INC.
440 Park Avenue South, New York, NY 10016 212-683-8960 Fax 212-213-1539
postmaster@dramatists.com www.dramatists.com

NEW PLAYS

★ **A CIVIL WAR CHRISTMAS: AN AMERICAN MUSICAL CELEBRA-TION by Paula Vogel, music by Daryl Waters.** It's 1864, and Washington, D.C. is settling down to the coldest Christmas Eve in years. Intertwining many lives, this musical shows us that the gladness of one's heart is the best gift of all. "Boldly inventive theater, warm and affecting." –*Talkin' Broadway.* "Crisp strokes of dialogue." –*NY Times.* [12M, 5W] ISBN: 978-0-8222-2361-0

★ **SPEECH & DEBATE by Stephen Karam.** Three teenage misfits in Salem, Oregon discover they are linked by a sex scandal that's rocked their town. "Savvy comedy." –*Variety.* "Hilarious, cliché-free, and immensely entertaining." –*NY Times.* "A strong, rangy play." –*NY Newsday.* [2M, 2W] ISBN: 978-0-8222-2286-6

★ **DIVIDING THE ESTATE by Horton Foote.** Matriarch Stella Gordon is determined not to divide her 100-year-old Texas estate, despite her family's declining wealth and the looming financial crisis. But her three children have another plan. "Goes for laughs and succeeds." –*NY Daily News.* "The theatrical equivalent of a page-turner." –*Bloomberg.com.* [4M, 9W] ISBN: 978-0-8222-2398-6

★ **WHY TORTURE IS WRONG, AND THE PEOPLE WHO LOVE THEM by Christopher Durang.** Christopher Durang turns political humor upside down with this raucous and provocative satire about America's growing homeland "insecurity." "A smashing new play." –*NY Observer.* "You may laugh yourself silly." –*Bloomberg News.* [4M, 3W] ISBN: 978-0-8222-2401-3

★ **FIFTY WORDS by Michael Weller.** While their nine-year-old son is away for the night on his first sleepover, Adam and Jan have an evening alone together, beginning a suspenseful nightlong roller-coaster ride of revelation, rancor, passion and humor. "Mr. Weller is a bold and productive dramatist." –*NY Times.* [1M, 1W] ISBN: 978-0-8222-2348-1

★ **BECKY'S NEW CAR by Steven Dietz.** Becky Foster is caught in middle age, middle management and in a middling marriage—with no prospects for change on the horizon. Then one night a socially inept and grief-struck millionaire stumbles into the car dealership where Becky works. "Gently and consistently funny." –*Variety.* "Perfect blend of hilarious comedy and substantial weight." –*Broadway Hour.* [4M, 3W] ISBN: 978-0-8222-2393-1

DRAMATISTS PLAY SERVICE, INC.
440 Park Avenue South, New York, NY 10016 212-683-8960 Fax 212-213-1539
postmaster@dramatists.com www.dramatists.com

NEW PLAYS

★ **AT HOME AT THE ZOO by Edward Albee.** Edward Albee delves deeper into his play THE ZOO STORY by adding a first act, HOMELIFE, which precedes Peter's fateful meeting with Jerry on a park bench in Central Park. "An essential and heartening experience." –*NY Times.* "Darkly comic and thrilling." –*Time Out.* "Genuinely fascinating." –*Journal News.* [2M, 1W] ISBN: 978-0-8222-2317-7

★ **PASSING STRANGE book and lyrics by Stew, music by Stew and Heidi Rodewald, created in collaboration with Annie Dorsen.** A daring musical about a young bohemian that takes you from black middle-class America to Amsterdam, Berlin and beyond on a journey towards personal and artistic authenticity. "Fresh, exuberant, bracingly inventive, bitingly funny, and full of heart." –*NY Times.* "The freshest musical in town!" –*Wall Street Journal.* "Excellent songs and a vulnerable heart." –*Variety.* [4M, 3W] ISBN: 978-0-8222-2400-6

★ **REASONS TO BE PRETTY by Neil LaBute.** Greg really, truly adores his girlfriend, Steph. Unfortunately, he also thinks she has a few physical imperfections, and when he mentions them, all hell breaks loose. "Tight, tense and emotionally true." –*Time Magazine.* "Lively and compulsively watchable." –*The Record.* [2M, 2W] ISBN: 978-0-8222-2394-8

★ **OPUS by Michael Hollinger.** With only a few days to rehearse a grueling Beethoven masterpiece, a world-class string quartet struggles to prepare their highest-profile performance ever—a televised ceremony at the White House. "Intimate, intense and profoundly moving." –*Time Out.* "Worthy of scores of bravissimos." –*BroadwayWorld.com.* [4M, 1W] ISBN: 978-0-8222-2363-4

★ **BECKY SHAW by Gina Gionfriddo.** When an evening calculated to bring happiness takes a dark turn, crisis and comedy ensue in this wickedly funny play that asks what we owe the people we love and the strangers who land on our doorstep. "As engrossing as it is ferociously funny." –*NY Times.* "Gionfriddo is some kind of genius." –*Variety.* [2M, 3W] ISBN: 978-0-8222-2402-0

★ **KICKING A DEAD HORSE by Sam Shepard.** Hobart Struther's horse has just dropped dead. In an eighty-minute monologue, he discusses what path brought him here in the first place, the fate of his marriage, his career, politics and eventually the nature of the universe. "Deeply instinctual and intuitive." –*NY Times.* "The brilliance is in the infinite reverberations Shepard extracts from his simple metaphor." –*TheaterMania.* [1M, 1W] ISBN: 978-0-8222-2336-8

DRAMATISTS PLAY SERVICE, INC.
440 Park Avenue South, New York, NY 10016 212-683-8960 Fax 212-213-1539
postmaster@dramatists.com www.dramatists.com

NEW PLAYS

★ **AUGUST: OSAGE COUNTY by Tracy Letts.** WINNER OF THE 2008 PULITZER PRIZE AND TONY AWARD. When the large Weston family reunites after Dad disappears, their Oklahoma homestead explodes in a maelstrom of repressed truths and unsettling secrets. "Fiercely funny and bitingly sad." *–NY Times.* "Ferociously entertaining." *–Variety.* "A hugely ambitious, highly combustible saga." *–NY Daily News.* [6M, 7W] ISBN: 978-0-8222-2300-9

★ **RUINED by Lynn Nottage.** WINNER OF THE 2009 PULITZER PRIZE. Set in a small mining town in Democratic Republic of Congo, RUINED is a haunting, probing work about the resilience of the human spirit during times of war. "A full-immersion drama of shocking complexity and moral ambiguity." *–Variety.* "Sincere, passionate, courageous." *–Chicago Tribune.* [8M, 4W] ISBN: 978-0-8222-2390-0

★ **GOD OF CARNAGE by Yasmina Reza, translated by Christopher Hampton.** WINNER OF THE 2009 TONY AWARD. A playground altercation between boys brings together their Brooklyn parents, leaving the couples in tatters as the rum flows and tensions explode. "Satisfyingly primitive entertainment." *–NY Times.* "Elegant, acerbic, entertainingly fueled on pure bile." *–Variety.* [2M, 2W] ISBN: 978-0-8222-2399-3

★ **THE SEAFARER by Conor McPherson.** Sharky has returned to Dublin to look after his irascible, aging brother. Old drinking buddies Ivan and Nicky are holed up at the house too, hoping to play some cards. But with the arrival of a stranger from the distant past, the stakes are raised ever higher. "Dark and enthralling Christmas fable." *–NY Times.* "A timeless classic." *–Hollywood Reporter.* [5M] ISBN: 978-0-8222-2284-2

★ **THE NEW CENTURY by Paul Rudnick.** When the playwright is Paul Rudnick, expectations are geared for a play both hilarious and smart, and this provocative and outrageous comedy is no exception. "The one-liners fly like rockets." *–NY Times.* "The funniest playwright around." *–Journal News.* [2M, 3W] ISBN: 978-0-8222-2315-3

★ **SHIPWRECKED! AN ENTERTAINMENT—THE AMAZING ADVENTURES OF LOUIS DE ROUGEMONT (AS TOLD BY HIMSELF) by Donald Margulies.** The amazing story of bravery, survival and celebrity that left nineteenth-century England spellbound. Dare to be whisked away. "A deft, literate narrative." *–LA Times.* "Springs to life like a theatrical pop-up book." *–NY Times.* [2M, 1W] ISBN: 978-0-8222-2341-2

DRAMATISTS PLAY SERVICE, INC.
440 Park Avenue South, New York, NY 10016 212-683-8960 Fax 212-213-1539
postmaster@dramatists.com www.dramatists.com